WHILE AMERICA SLEPT

RESTORING AMERICAN LEADERSHIP TO A WORLD IN CRISIS

Robert C. O'Brien

FOREWORD BY HUGH HEWITT

ENCOUNTER BOOKS
New York • London

First American edition published in 2016 by Encounter Books,
an activity of Encounter for Culture and Education, Inc.,
a nonprofit, tax exempt corporation.
Encounter Books website address: www.encounterbooks.com

Manufactured in the United States and printed on
acid-free paper. The paper used in this publication meets
the minimum requirements of ANSI/NISO Z39.48-1992
(R 1997) (*Permanence of Paper*).

FIRST AMERICAN EDITION

LIBRARY OF CONGRESS CATALOGING-IN-PUBLICATION DATA
Names: O'Brien, Robert C., 1966– author.
Title: While America slept : restoring American leadership to a world in crisis /
by Robert C. O'Brien ; foreword by Hugh Hewitt.
Description: New York : Encounter Books, [2016] |
Includes bibliographical references and index.
Identifiers: LCCN 2016007354 (print) | LCCN 2016019473 (ebook) |
ISBN 9781594039034 (hardcover : alk. paper) | ISBN 9781594039041 (Ebook)
Subjects: LCSH: United States—Foreign relations—21st century. |
National security—United States. | United States—Military policy.
Classification: LCC JZ1480 .O37 2016 (print) | LCC JZ1480 (ebook) |
DDC 355/.033573—dc23
LC record available at https://lccn.loc.gov/2016007354
Interior page design and composition: BooksByBruce.com

Advance Praise for *While America Slept*

Robert O'Brien is well known as an expert on naval affairs but this book shows a penetrating understanding of the broad range of national security issues. It's a must-read for anyone who wants to know how and why the threats to America are growing, and what we can do about them.

– SENATOR JIM TALENT

No president in the history of the United States, not even Jimmy Carter, has been as disastrous to America's national security interests, global standing, and foreign policy as Barack Obama. From the rise of ISIS to the resurgence of Russia, Obama and his team didn't see any of it coming—but Robert O'Brien did. All of it. As one of America's most important national security and foreign policy voices, O'Brien is continually one step ahead of global events and informed to an astounding depth. His captivating essays succinctly outline the challenges our nation faces and what we must do to surmount them. Imagine the brilliance of Kissinger combined with the talent of Clancy and you have only scratched the surface of Robert O'Brien's writing. These essays are absolute must-reads for anyone who cares about the future of the United States.

– BRAD THOR, #1 *NEW YORK TIMES* BESTSELLING AUTHOR
OF *CODE OF CONDUCT*

When Robert writes on a national security issue, people pay attention. He knows how to cut through the clutter to highlight the problem and articulate a solution. He also knows when others aren't confronting the real issues and holds the powerful accountable.

– RICHARD GRENELL, FOX NEWS CONTRIBUTOR

Robert O'Brien has made a strong contribution to the American dialogue about our national security and the particular role that maritime power has to play in our nation's future. Well worth the read for serious thinkers.

– DR. JERRY HENDRIX, CAPTAIN, UNITED STATES NAVY (RET.)

In a time when America's foreign policy seems to have become the province of amateurs and cynical former campaign volunteers, a voice like Robert O'Brien's is a breath of fresh air. A go-to lawyer in high-stakes litigation, a seasoned diplomat, and an Army Reserve officer, Robert's take on the issues hearkens back to the time when United States foreign policy was in the hands of wise, accomplished, experienced adults who understood the stakes because they had lived lives outside of graduate school seminars and away from computer screens. Someday America will again be ready to embrace maturity when it comes to national security, and Robert O'Brien will be on the short list of wise men and women who will rebuild America's stature in the world. While America Slept will be a blueprint for that critical reconstruction.

– KURT SCHLICHTER, AUTHOR, ATTORNEY, AND COLONEL,
UNITED STATES ARMY (RET.)

For Robert Christopher O'Brien

TABLE OF CONTENTS

FOREWORD

ANSWER: "Because national security is different."

QUESTION: "I never read 'collections' of articles unless they were authored by Charles Krauthammer, Peggy Noonan, or George Will. Why should I read one where all the pieces are by a 'super-lawyer' I've never heard of?"

The answer above is all you need to know. "We have no permanent allies," Britain's great Victorian-era Prime Minister and global strategist Lord Palmerston is said to have declared. "We have no permanent enemies; we have only permanent interests."

Some dispute whether "Palmy" actually said this—but no matter. He ought to have said it because he conducted Great Britain's foreign policy as though he believed it with every fiber of his being. So have all the greatest national security strategists. So will the national security strategists that seek to recover America's badly damaged position in the world.

Because America's "permanent interests" have been badly damaged by the past seven years of maladministration, the best thinking about what should have been done during those years is now vitally important to inform the decisions to be made for the next eight years, beginning with whom Americans pick to replace the worst foreign policy president since Jimmy Carter.

In 1978, right in the middle of the locust years that made up the Carter presidency, I graduated from college and went to work for former President Richard Nixon in his exile in San Clemente, California, as second to head writer Ray Price on the project that would emerge in the spring of 1980 titled *The Real War*. Nixon wrote *The Real War* with the purpose of directly impacting the presidential campaign in which, for obvious reasons, he could have no visible part. But Ronald Reagan was photographed carrying *The Real War* about and we felt our work had been done. A book read and timely displayed is both crucial content for the campaign and a marker of a candidate's seriousness.

Robert C. O'Brien's collection of essays on national security from the Obama years and his new introduction serve the same purpose as Nixon's 1980 book did. Of course, O'Brien has none of Nixon's notoriety, and with good reason—he has served quietly as a diplomat and lawyer in some of the world's most dangerous places and usually out of the spotlight. In the George W. Bush administration he advised Ambassador John Bolton at the UN and headed a State Department initiative to build the rule of law in Afghanistan. He was a close advisor to Mitt Romney in two presidential campaigns. He has monitored elections in Georgia and Ukraine and briefed many GOP presidential hopefuls on the needs of the Department of Defense generally and the US Navy specifically.

O'Brien is in such demand among the GOP presidential campaigns that not one but two "O'Brien primaries" were held in 2015. The first took place when Governor Romney decided not to run. Governor Walker then delivered clear calls for rearmament before his campaign ended—calls shaped by O'Brien and his fellow realist and friend, former Missouri Senator Jim Talent. No sooner had Governor Walker withdrawn from the race than O'Brien's phone began ringing a second time with requests that he join this or that national security team. Instead of committing to any of the candidates, O'Brien decided to commit to them all via this book and an output of key pieces and features on the national security challenges facing the next president.

In our lifetimes, Republican presidents have arrived at 1600 Pennsylvania Avenue tasked with clearing away the rubble of collapsed national security strategies three times: Nixon in 1969, Reagan in 1980, and George W. Bush in 2001. "W" inherited a perilously threat-blind national security situation, but even as 9/11 loomed and the new team scrambled to make sense of the chaos left behind by President Clinton, there were strong and able men and women rushing to fill gaps. The attacks left the country devastated, but America rebounded, and with a ferocity that struck the world, led the crushing of the alliance between the Taliban and al-Qaeda, the toppling of Saddam, and the stripping from Qaddafi of all his WMD—thank God. Not long after came unheralded but crucial strategic alliances in Africa, the expansion of NATO, and a strategic understanding with China that was, if not warm, at least stable.

Israel was secure and strongly supported when George W. Bush left office. A tenuous but potentially lasting peace had been won in Iraq through the surge and the sacrifices of the American military. Russia and Iran were contained and the latter was breaking under comprehensive sanctions. The American military was strong and deployed on every front where it was needed. America had a strategic vision—it was being implemented and it was working.

Then came a financial panic not seen since 1907. It crashed the election of 2008 and took America's collective eyes off the dangers around the globe. As Federal Reserve Chairman Ben Bernanke recounted in his 2015 memoir *The Courage To Act,* financial crises were occurring almost weekly throughout the fall of 2008, and the election of President Obama was almost certainly a response to the fear and uncertainty in markets during that time. Sadly, the new president was perhaps the least well equipped in history to manage a strategically complicated and increasingly dangerous world. Though many millions do not yet understand this, the consequences of his amateurism combined with the (genuinely) killer instincts of Vladimir Putin, the relentlessness of both the People's Republic of China and the Islamic Republic of Iran, and the bloodlust of Islamist extremists have been catastrophic for the United States.

Just as the blinders of the late Clinton years that kept America from seeing the threat growing in Afghanistan, the domestic political antics of President Obama and a paralyzed Congress have blinded large swaths of America to the new threats that loom in 2016 as large as those that gathered in 2000.

Thus, this timely book from a man recognized across the center-right as among the leading thinkers on global strategy in the rising generation. The Kissingers and the Schultzes, who served so long and so well, still can sally forth with a burst of strategic clarity, but a new generation of strategists is emerging that will guide America's rebuilding of its alliances and its military, and especially its doctrines of engagement.

O'Brien's book could not be more vital at this moment in history. He invites the reader to revisit the issues that have followed one upon the other over the past eight years and take away a deep understanding of the sheer number and scale of challenges facing the next president. Don't be surprised if O'Brien emerges as the key voice and guiding hand of a new and serious National Security Council in the West Wing, or at the

Departments of Defense or State in 2017. The new president will need him and the expertise he details here. But no one man or woman can get the job done alone. Scores and scores of serious, sacrifice-minded patriots need to stand in many gaps. Those interested in so serving can get a start by absorbing the key facts and lessons from each of these essays.

We read old things—as old as Thucydides' account of the Melians' appeal to the Athenians in the *History of the Peloponnesian War*—to inform future decision making on American national security matters, because as Lord Palmerston indicated 150 years ago, states have permanent interests, not permanent strategic situations. These old things inform us best when they are written well and persuasively, and remain quite obviously relevant to the headlines of today, as O'Brien's essays are. Take this new introduction and collection and absorb it for the fall campaign and beyond. It will certainly be read in foreign capitals where O'Brien's reputation and views are already well known. We can only hope every would-be GOP nominee dives deeply into these pages, and with them, tens of thousands of influencers and serious voters. The country needs a dose of realism about the threats surrounding it. O'Brien's book is part of a "wake-up" series of alarms that need sounding.

HUGH HEWITT
IRVINE, CALIFORNIA
MAY 10, 2016

PREFACE

On January 20, 2009, the United States inaugurated a new President with high hopes for the future and genuine good will—even from his political opponents. President Barack Obama had promised to transform America and the world. Within less than a year, the Nobel Prize was awarded to him on the basis of that promise alone. Seven years into his administration, there can be no question that he has succeeded in his transformational aspirations. In 2016, the world is a very different place than the one that existed when Mr. Obama was elected.

President Obama took office by telling America's adversaries in his inaugural address that "we will extend a hand if you are willing to unclench your fist." At a NATO summit in April of the same year, he redefined traditional notions of American exceptionalism by stating: "I believe in American exceptionalism, just as I suspect that the Brits believe in British exceptionalism and the Greeks believe in Greek exceptionalism." He told Europeans that "there have been times where America has shown arrogance and been dismissive, even derisive." In Turkey, he said, "[t]he United States is still working through some of our own darker periods in our history." He noted that "[o]ur country still struggles with the legacies of slavery and segregation, the past treatment of Native Americans." In Cairo, he claimed that "fear and anger" from 9/11 "led us to act contrary to our traditions and our ideals."

President Obama, as he boasted in January 2012, personally guided the process by which the United States massively cut its defense budget, yielding the smallest Army, Navy, and Marine Corps since before World War II. He said he would use the savings to "pay down our debt, and... to rebuild America." Instead, the US budget deficit soared. I am certain he believed other nations would follow suit and engage in their own rounds of disarmament. They did not.

President Obama's statements and actions suggest that he may have agreed with former diplomat Francis Fukuyama, who wrote in 1989, following the collapse of Communism, that "what we may be witnessing is not just the end of the Cold War…but…the end point of mankind's ideological evolution and the universalization of Western liberal democracy as the final form of human government." I have no doubt that President Obama truly believed that by reaching out to our adversaries with humility and concessions, by acknowledging America's sins and minimizing her historic role as an exceptional nation, and by unilaterally and drastically reducing her defense capability, he would earn goodwill and reciprocity from those he himself had labeled "corrupt and deceitful" leaders. Instead, the autocrats, tyrants, and terrorists were emboldened. China, Russia, and Iran engaged in significant arms buildups even as America drew down, cutting into and perhaps eliminating our military edge. At the same time, by force or threat thereof, in some cases using proxies, these nations grabbed territory in the South China Sea, Eastern Europe, and across the Middle East. At the same time, a well-organized Islamic terrorist group—ISIS—established a caliphate throughout vast swaths of territory in Iraq and Syria.

President Obama's thinking is not new. America's former ambassador to the United Nations, Jeane Kirkpatrick, addressed it in her famous speech to the Republican National Convention in Dallas on August 20, 1984. I remember it well, as I was fortunate enough to hear it from the convention floor where I was serving as a page. She called those that looked away from Soviet aggression and Iranian terrorism and found fault instead with US policy the "blame America first crowd." She noted the wisdom of the "American people [who] know that it's dangerous to blame ourselves for terrible problems that we did not cause."

As a lawyer with an international practice and as an advisor to Republican presidential candidates Mitt Romney, Scott Walker, and Ted Cruz, my travels have taken me to regions of the world that are in turmoil. I have seen firsthand the consequences of what the Obama White House itself calls the President's "lead from behind" foreign policy. Since President Obama was sworn in, I have been to Afghanistan, Guantánamo Bay, Ukraine, the Republic of Georgia, Estonia, Israel, the Persian Gulf states, and various nations in Southeast Asia and Africa. In each of these places, the fallout of what *Wall Street Journal* editor Bret Stephens describes as "America in retreat" is apparent—and it is sad.

In Afghanistan, some young Afghan patriots, who chose to side with us after the 9/11 attacks, asked me if we would abandon their country as we had abandoned Iraq. At the American naval station in Guantánamo Bay, I sat next to the family members of 9/11 victims and watched as Khalid Sheikh Mohammed and his co-conspirators were led into a civilized courtroom to be defended by the best lawyers in America for their unspeakable acts of mass murder. As they watched the perpetrators of evil carry in their prayer rugs and beads, the family members wondered: Would the terrorists ever face justice for their crimes? Would they be moved to America and be given even more rights and more lenient incarceration, or possibly, would they even be released onto our streets?

In Kiev, Ukraine, my translator, a newly minted lawyer, explained to me that he and his friends were forced to crowdsource body armor when one of their college buddies volunteered to go to the eastern front to fight Russian regulars. He asked if the United States could send some of the Kevlar vests we were no longer using in Iraq to his friends. A reasonable request, but one which we have not satisfactorily answered. The Ukrainians are willing to fight for their own freedom—but unlike freedom fighters in the past, they have little access to the arsenal of democracy.

When I monitored polls for the free and fair presidential election in the Republic of Georgia, my driver had to take us on a circuitous route away from the frontlines in South Ossetia. He did this because Russian soldiers take pot shots from time to time at Georgians who get too close to the artificial border created by Vladimir Putin. Whether it is Ukraine, the Caucasus, Central Asia, the Baltics or, now, Syria, the Russian bear is on the move and the American eagle studiously looks away.

I have stood in a Kibbutz kindergarten in Israel near the border with Gaza that was shelled with Hamas' Qassam rockets. I saw the Hezbollah entrenchments in Southern Lebanon from a watchtower in the Golan Heights. Our Israeli hosts struggled to understand the Obama administration's naïve hope that Iran, which sponsors both Hamas and Hezbollah, would somehow become America's geopolitical partner in the Middle East. In what is certainly the worst diplomatic deal since Munich,

President Obama has paved the way for a nuclear Iran and given the mullahs over $100 billion dollars in sanctions relief as an incentive to agree to Western appeasement.

America's closest ally in the Gulf is Kuwait. Twenty-six years after Saddam's invasion and occupation of their country, the people of Kuwait remain grateful to the United States and United Kingdom and to President Bush and Prime Ministers Thatcher and Major for standing up for the principle that the powerful should not be able to change their borders at the expense of the weak. Businessmen with whom I spoke were incredulous that America had supported Mohammed Morsi and his Muslim Brotherhood followers as they attempted a rolling coup in Egypt. When General Sisi was elected President of Egypt on a platform of rooting out Islamic extremism, Washington was indifferent at best and hostile at worst. The Gulf Arabs were truly taken aback by such an approach to the clear and present danger of radical Islamists controlling the Arab world's largest country and its cultural hub.

In Southeast Asia and Africa, the biggest untold story of the new century is the rise of China. For example, in one small Southeast Asian country, a land that owes its very existence to Western humanitarian intervention, China built the nation's new Ministry of Defense building. It also seeks to install powerful radar systems to track the movement of American and allied shipping in the South Pacific. Throughout Africa, from Cape Town to Addis Ababa, China is building roads and government buildings and laying fiber-optic cables. It will soon control the continent's infrastructure, mining, and agricultural sectors and even maintain military bases in harbors that were once famous ports of call for Western navies. Over two million Chinese nationals live in Africa and some argue that Africa is undergoing a stealth recolonization, this time directed from Beijing.

I have negotiated in Beijing with senior Chinese government officials. They appear entirely confident that America and the West are in decline, and that the twenty-first century will be theirs. Whether it is in the economic, cyber, military, or political arenas, China no longer bides its time. It creates artificial islands in the South China Sea that the White House orders the US Navy to avoid. It establishes an Air Identification Zone over Japanese-administered islands in the East China Sea that foreign—including American—airlines respect. It hacks the most personal data of every American that has served in the military or government without any repercussions. And it vetoes American-led human rights initiatives in international organizations without consequence.

Bill Clinton's former Secretary of State, Madeleine Albright, has surveyed a world transformed by President Obama's policies and called it "a mess." Robert Kagan looks at the "world America made" and fears that we may be watching it "drift away." Less than four years ago Mitt Romney was mocked for warning of the rise of Islamic extremism in the Middle East and Africa and the resurgence of our long time geopolitical foe, Russia. Now even progressive publications ask, "Was Mitt right about everything?" Albright, Kagan, and Romney are all correct in their analysis. Frighteningly, at the same time that the world becomes ever more dangerous, this administration is decimating America's unparalleled armed forces.

I have embarked with our courageous young sailors and aviators on the aircraft carrier *USS John C. Stennis* and visited our cutting-edge Virginia-class submarines and Arleigh Burke-class destroyers. I walked the floors of one of the last subcontractors with the capacity to manufacture key components for those destroyers. Although our sailors and their equipment are still the best in the world, the United States Navy is in crisis. It is too small already and, under the Obama administration's sequestration program, will shrink further. Given the demands with which we have tasked them, our sailors and their ships are stressed and stretched to the readiness breaking point. Some of our newer warships would be out-gunned by those of our competitors. Unless sequestration ends soon, our shipbuilding industrial base may wither to the extent that the next president will be unable to rebuild the fleet without purchasing warships from foreign contractors.

Unfortunately, it is not just the Navy that is suffering. President Obama's hand-picked Undersecretary of Defense for Personnel and Readiness recently said that the Army is at its smallest size since before World War II. If the cuts go any deeper, he stated, "they will become a matter of grave worry to us all." The Marine Corps faces similar personnel cuts and is short of amphibious ships and landing craft to deliver them to the littoral battlefields. The Air Force is stretched so thin that America can no longer take air superiority for granted. If the mainstay of our bomber force, the B-52, were a person, it would qualify for Social

Security. The service claims it can no longer afford the critical close air support provided by the A-10. It is unlikely that the service will ever receive enough of the over-budget F-35 Joint Strike Fighters to replace its current squadrons of F-15 and F-16 jet fighters.

In the 1930s, Winston Churchill, out of cabinet office and exiled to the political wilderness, saw the rising menace of the totalitarian regimes that would eventually form the axis powers. With little influence within the Conservative Party or Parliament, he went to the British people directly, through articles and speeches, to warn of the gathering storm. His prescient speeches were published in book form in 1938. The United States edition was aptly titled, *While England Slept*. His anthology of articles published the next year was chillingly called, *Step by Step*.

While it would be entirely immodest to compare this book or any of my writings to those of Sir Winston, he has long been a hero of mine in an Anglo-American pantheon that includes Washington, Lincoln, Reagan, and Thatcher. Churchill's writings and speeches were what first inspired me to enter the editorial fray and write short pieces about the challenges I saw in my international travels and in my political work. This book is a compilation of those articles. Like this preface, the essays warn of the dangers that America faces, and how we should respond to them.

The United States must resume its role as the leader of the free world. Only in such a leadership role can America, as John F. Kennedy stated, "assure the survival and the success of liberty."

To effectively lead and preserve peace, America must rebuild its defenses. Ronald Reagan believed, as did our ancient Roman forebears, that "we maintain the peace through our strength; weakness only invites aggression." He was right, and his policy of "peace through strength" led to a decisive American victory in the Cold War. In the face of rising challenges around the world, it is time to return to a national security policy based on "peace through strength." A strong America will be a nation that our allies will trust and our adversaries will not dare test. Only under those conditions will the United States lead the world in assuring the survival and success of liberty.

President Obama has indeed transformed America during his term in office. The country and the world have paid a heavy price for his approach to domestic and foreign policy. I remain, however, optimistic about our future. I am grateful to live in the United States at this time. I grew up in small-town America where the Fourth of July was celebrated with almost the same enthusiasm as Christmas. It was marked by block parties, bottle rockets, and parades. My friends and I had fathers and grandfathers and great-grandfathers who had worn the uniforms of our nation's armed forces.

We knew that America was a winning nation. We also knew that when America won, free people around the world won. Although we grew up in the shadow of Vietnam, Watergate, and the Carter years—including the humiliating Iranian hostage crisis—we knew that America would come back. In 1980, Ronald Reagan was elected president and our country and the world witnessed a rebirth of freedom that many believed they would never see. I am certain that that American people still believe in winning; that they still see our land as the "shining city upon a hill." I am confident that the United States of America will make another such comeback—and that it will be soon.

ROBERT C. O'BRIEN
LOS ANGELES, CALIFORNIA
MAY 10, 2016

INTRODUCTION

When Russia annexed Crimea and invaded Ukraine in February and March of 2014, I immediately thought back to Christmas Eve 1979, when the Soviet Union invaded Afghanistan. This was the first direct use of Soviet troops outside the Eastern Bloc since World War II, "a watershed event of the Cold War."[1] Much like the Obama administration today, the Carter administration was already reeling from a series of foreign policy failures. As historian John Lewis Gaddis wrote, the invasion was "only the most dramatic of a series of humiliations for the United States."[2] The Soviets had deployed nuclear missiles to Europe in 1977 and Soviet-backed Cuban troops had intervened in Angola in 1975 and Ethiopia and Zaire in 1977. The Iranian revolution and subsequent hostage crisis, the rise of the Soviet-backed Sandinistas in Nicaragua, and the Vietnamese invasion of Cambodia added to the general sense of crisis.

In a preview of President Obama's wishful-thinking foreign policy approach, President Carter initially refused to confront Soviet aggression. Just a year before the invasion, a communist coup in Kabul had ended hopes of a more constructive relationship between the United States and Afghanistan. Carter's National Security Advisor, Zbigniew Brzezinski, recommended cutting diplomatic ties, but Carter rejected his advice and, siding with the State Department, recognized the new pro-Soviet government. Shortly thereafter, the new US ambassador to Afghanistan was assassinated in February 1979. (The next United States ambassador to be assassinated would be J. Christopher Stevens in Benghazi, Libya on

---

1 US Department of State, Office of the Historian, "Milestones: 1977–1980" (Washington, DC: US Department of State, October 31, 2013), https://history.state.gov/milestones/1977-1980/soviet-invasion-afghanistan.
2 John Lewis Gaddis, *Strategies of Containment: A Critical Appraisal of American National Security Policy during the Cold War* (Oxford, England: Oxford University Press, 1982), http://www.amazon.com/Strategies-Containment-Critical-Appraisal-American/dp/019517447X.

Portions of this introduction appeared in the *National Interest*, December 26, 2015.

September 11, 2012.) Yet President Carter was still holding on to the hopes of détente. He was determined, as he had earlier told Leonid Brezhnev, "to improve relations with the Soviet Union on the basis of reciprocity, mutual respect, and advantage."[3]

The Soviet invasion of Afghanistan shocked Carter into changing course. Six days after the invasion, Carter admitted that his "opinion of the Russians has changed more drastically in the last week than even the previous two and a half years before that." Addressing Congress the following month, Carter described the Soviet move as the "most serious threat to peace since the Second World War."[4] Carter authorized increased lethal military support to the Afghan mujahedeen, withdrew the SALT II treaty from Senate consideration, cancelled grain exports to the Soviet Union, restricted trade in strategic items, led a controversial boycott of the Moscow Olympics, and articulated the "Carter Doctrine" to protect the Persian Gulf from outside (i.e., Soviet) interference. Most importantly, Carter began a defense buildup that was further accelerated by Ronald Reagan.

Today, Republicans often call President Obama the worst foreign policy president since Jimmy Carter. But it is increasingly clear this comparison is unfair to Carter. Faced with a series of foreign policy challenges, Carter was willing to admit his previous approach was not working and take steps, in his words, to "make the Soviets pay for their unwarranted aggression."[5]

President Obama has shown no such urgency or adaptability. Faced with a resurgent Russia, an assertive China that has claimed sovereignty over an entire swath of the Pacific Ocean, the rise of ISIS, the related "apocalyptic disaster" in Syria,[6] a nuclear-threshold Iran, and increasing threats to the homeland from radical Islamic terrorism, President Obama simply refuses to change course. Instead, the president labels his critics

---

3 "Carter-Brezhnev Letters, January–February 1977," http://astro.temple.edu/~rimmerma/Carter_Brezhnev_letters.htm.

4 President Jimmy Carter, "State of the Union Address" (The American Presidency Project, January 23, 1980), http://www.presidency.ucsb.edu/ws/?pid=33079.

5 Keren Yarki-Milo, *Knowing the Adversary: Leaders, Intelligence, and Assessment of Intentions in International Relations* (Princeton, NJ: Princeton University Press, 2014), http://tinyurl.com/gnftgsu.

6 Christopher M. Blanchard et al., "Armed Conflict in Syria: Overview and US Response" (Washington, DC: Congressional Research Service, October 9, 2015), https://www.fas.org/sgp/crs/mideast/RL33487.pdf.

"neocons,"[7] sets up a straw-man choice between his "lead from behind" policies and all-out war, distances himself from key allies, and apologizes to or weakly negotiates with our adversaries.

Asked in August 2015 what lessons he'd learned from recent crises, President Obama said, "There's no doubt that, after six and a half years, I am that much more confident in the assessments I make and can probably see around the corners faster than I did when I first came into office." He went on: "And I am confirmed in my belief that much of the time, we are making judgments based on percentages, and ... there are always going to be some complications ... so maybe at the same time as I'm more confident today, I'm also more humble."

During that same six-and-a-half years, I have warned about the growing threats to America and her allies. Section 1 of this book considers the consequences of President Obama's "lead from behind" isolationist foreign policy. Sadly, friend and foe alike can only conclude that America is currently a nation in retreat. Sections 2 and 3 focus on the decline in the nation's military capability under this president's defense sequestration program, especially as it relates to the United States Navy, America's primary tool for maintaining "presence" and projecting power throughout the world. While disarmament has long been a goal of the "blame America first" crowd, there can be no doubt that abandonment of a "peace through strength" military posture has made the world a more dangerous place. Section 4 discusses the rise of America's closest "peer competitor"—China. Taking advantage of a United States that is in retreat and intent on cutting its military budget, China is positioning itself to become a superpower. Section 5 reviews several discrete aspects of the global war on terror—a war that President Obama refuses to acknowledge is a war and which he had naïvely hoped to end through a series of apologies and retreats. Section 6 provides encouragement to the Grand Old Party showing that, notwithstanding the drumbeat from the mainstream media that demographics give the Democrats a lock on the White House, there is a bright future for Republicans. In an epilogue, I outline several policies that the new president can implement to return America to its rightful and critical role as the leader of the free world.

---

7 President Barack Obama, "Press Conference," Antalya, Turkey, November 16, 2015, https://www. whitehouse.gov/the-press-office/2015/11/16/press-conference-president-obama-antalya-turkey.

Following the Soviet invasion of Afghanistan, President Carter told the nation on January 4, 1980: "History teaches, perhaps, very few clear lessons. But surely one such lesson learned by the world at great cost is that aggression, unopposed, becomes a contagious disease."[8] President Ronald Reagan, Carter's successor, understood that lesson well. Through strong leadership, close collaboration with American allies and like-minded leaders such as Prime Minister Thatcher and Pope John Paul II, and by rebuilding the United States military to forcefully deter aggression, he won the Cold War, bringing freedom to millions of people around the world.

Sadly, in the face of Russian aggression, Chinese expansionism, and Islamic extremism from both ISIS and the Islamic Republic of Iran, this is a lesson that President Obama refuses to learn. His successor will inherit a world in crisis that will require robust and strategic American leadership. The good news is that while America slept during the Obama years, a new president, willing to lead, can usher in another "morning in America." That is good for our country and for the world.

---

8 President Jimmy Carter, "Address to the Nation on the Soviet Invasion of Afghanistan" (The American Presidency Project, January 4, 1980), http://www.presidency.ucsb.edu/ws/?pid=33079. http://www.presidency.ucsb.edu/ws/?pid=32911.

SECTION 1

America 2016
A Nation in Retreat

What Would Winston Churchill Do?

Russia's naked grab of Crimea, its continuing intimidation of Kiev, and Putin's proffered justification—that he is merely protecting ethnic Russians—parallel a much darker time in European history. Former Secretary of State Hillary Clinton made this point: "Now if this sounds familiar, it's what Hitler did back in the '30s. All the Germans that were ... the ethnic Germans, the Germans by ancestry who were in places like Czechoslovakia and Romania and other places, Hitler kept saying, 'they're not being treated right. I must go and protect my people,' and that's what's gotten everybody so nervous."

In the Pacific, China has not undertaken military action as dramatic as the Russian invasion of Crimea but it has staked a claim to almost the entirety of the South China Sea with its "nine-dash line." In the process, China's Navy and Coast Guard have expelled the Philippines from the Scarborough Shoal, a reef just under 150 miles from the Philippines but almost 550 miles from Hainan Island, the nearest Chinese port. Responding to American and regional concerns raised about China's position on the South China Sea, Foreign Minister Yang Jiechi proclaimed in July 2010, "China is a big country and other countries are small countries, and that's just a fact."

This article was originally published in the *National Interest*, April 11, 2014.

China is also actively contesting long-time Japanese administration of the Senkaku Islands in the East China Sea, and it unilaterally imposed an Air Defense Identification Zone covering waters and islands administered by both Japan and South Korea. It is widely reported that the West's lack of response to Russia's Crimean adventure has spooked America's Pacific allies, particularly Japan. These allies believe the lesson China has drawn from the situation is that the West would likewise countenance a military resolution of its territorial claims.

While regional powers have unsuccessfully sought to conquer their neighbors in recent decades—most notably Argentina's invasion and occupation of the Falklands in 1982 and Iraq's invasion and occupation of Kuwait in 1991—the major powers have eschewed such conduct since China's 1951 annexation of Tibet. Given events in Ukraine and the Pacific, that long period of relative stability appears to be at an end, notwithstanding President Obama's comment following Russia's invasion of Crimea, "because you're bigger and stronger taking a piece of the country—that is not how international law and international norms are observed in the twenty-first century."

To the contrary, Putin's and China's actions declare, the new "international norms" look alarmingly like those of eight decades ago.

The authoritarian powers, Russia and China, have the initiative and are on the move. They are, in turn, watched by a regional provocateur, Iran, which has its own visions of Middle Eastern hegemony. The Western European democracies and Japan, after years of slashing defense budgets, are ill prepared to face these challenges. Under the Obama administration, America joined the disarmament club through sequestration. Even in the face of the Russia's invasion of Crimea, the administration plans to mothball half of the Navy's robust cruiser fleet. Secretary Hagel talked of doing something similar to the carrier fleet, while at the same time cutting many thousands of troops from the Army and Marines, respectively. Pollsters claim American voters are exhausted by the wars in Iraq and Afghanistan and show little interest in foreign conflicts. Following public opinion, rather than leading it, Western leaders are wary of intervening in any substantial manner on behalf of small, faraway nations such as Ukraine or the Philippines.

Given the echoes of the 1930s we hear today, it is useful to review the events of 1938. Austria was annexed into the German Third Reich on

March 12, 1938. The annexation took place the day after agitation by the Austrian Nazi Party and German demands—swiftly followed by German invasion—ousted the legitimate government in Vienna. A referendum on the union between Austria and Germany—scheduled for the next day— was cancelled. A month later, the Germans held their own referendum; under the watchful eyes of the Wehrmacht and without ballot secrecy, Austrians voted for union. The Anschluss took place a few months before the twentieth anniversary of the German surrender in World War I and violated Germany's post-war treaty obligations. Interestingly, Russia's annexation of Crimea took place just twenty-three years after the dissolution of the Soviet Union, an event Putin has labeled the "greatest geopolitical catastrophe of the century."

Two weeks following the Anschluss, Winston Churchill strode into the British House of Commons and stated: "[A] country like ours, possessed of immense territory and wealth, whose defenses have been neglected, cannot avoid war by dilating upon its horrors, or even by a continuous display of pacific qualities, or by ignoring the fate of the victims of aggression elsewhere. War will be avoided, in present circumstances, only by the accumulation of deterrents against the aggressor." He continued:

> I have watched this famous island descending incontinently, feck-lessly the stairway which leads to a dark gulf … If mortal catastrophe should overtake the British nation and the British Empire, historians a thousand years hence will still be baffled by the mystery of our affairs. They will never understand how it was that a victorious nation, with everything in hand, suffered themselves to be brought low and to cast away all that they had gained by measureless sacrifice and absolute victory—gone with the wind!

A quarter-century after the end of the Cold War, similar words could certainly be used to describe America's present circumstances—but there is no Commons debating such matters and no Churchill thundering warnings of what may lie ahead. Back in 1938, the pace of events quickened, and by the end of September the great powers were agreeing to strip Czechoslovakia's strategic industrial and banking regions from the country without its consent, awarding the so-called Sudetenland to the

Third Reich in a further effort to slake Hitler's thirst for conquest and avoid a Europe-wide war.

While the majority of Britons supported Prime Minister Neville Chamberlain's appeasement of Hitler as an act of statesmanship in the pursuit of peace, Churchill, back in the Commons on October 5, laid out the truth of the matter: "All is over. Silent, mournful, abandoned, broken, Czechoslovakia recedes into the darkness. She has suffered in every respect by her association with the Western democracies and with the League of Nations, of which she has always been an obedient servant."

Churchill acknowledged the popularity of Chamberlain's appeasement but correctly labeled it a defeat:

> I do not grudge our loyal, brave people, who were ready to do their duty no matter what the cost, who never flinched under the strain of last week—I do not grudge them the natural, spontaneous outburst of joy and relief when they learned that the hard ordeal would no longer be required of them at the moment; but they should know the truth. They should know that there has been gross neglect and deficiency in our defenses; they should know that we have sustained a defeat without a war the consequences of which will travel far with us along our road …

Churchill then prophetically warned his countrymen and his audience across the Atlantic of the consequences of the appeasement policy: "And do not suppose that this is the end. This is only the beginning of the reckoning. This is only the first sip, the first foretaste of a bitter cup which will be proffered to us year by year unless by a supreme recovery of moral health and martial vigor, we arise again and take our stand for freedom as in the olden time."

After a decade of disarmament followed by appeasement, Hitler invaded Poland in September 1939—swiftly followed by Stalin, who sought to secure his share of the spoils. Fortunately, the United Kingdom and its allies were able to turn to the man who had foretold of the calamity and who possessed the courage and fortitude to hold the forces of darkness at bay during that perilous time while what remained of the free world frantically rearmed to meet the challenge. Having given the warning for so many years, Churchill alone had the credibility to rally the British people and eventually the English-speaking peoples.

It is the sincere hope of all men and women of good will that the recent events in Europe and the Pacific are not, in fact, the first sip of another "bitter cup," and that the authoritarian regimes will retreat from the use of force or even the threat thereof against their neighbors— whether it be for territorial conquest or to exert influence over them. There are too many Western leaders willing to play Chamberlain's role today. Governor Mitt Romney's Churchill-like warning of a resurgent Russia, made during the 2012 campaign, was mocked by the president and elites and rejected by a narrow margin at the polls. Perhaps because of that example, very few elected officials have been willing to speak bluntly about this gathering storm. From the sidelines, Romney continues to do so, and Senator Marco Rubio and Ambassador John Bolton have delivered speeches with the unpopular message that vigor and hard choices are required of us if we are to arise and take our stand for freedom. The media elites refuse to face the realities of the world, however, and it will take sustained, disciplined rhetoric from credible voices to wake the West, the world, and even peaceful elements within the authoritarian regimes—especially commercially savvy and modern China—to the dangers of this old new era. ∎

=⇒ | ⇐=

Obama's Folly
The Iran Deal Disaster

In a recent press conference, President Obama said that his deal with Iran is the best outcome that could be achieved. History proves otherwise. Unlike past successful nonproliferation efforts with respect to states seeking nuclear weapons, this deal moves Iran further down the path toward obtaining a nuclear weapon. Indeed, the deal actually recognizes Iran's "right" to enrich uranium and Iran will keep at least five thousand nuclear centrifuges spinning into the future. Six previous United Nations Security Council resolutions stated the opposite. Iran flouted those resolutions and is now being rewarded for its clandestine and illegal nuclear enrichment activity.

When South Africa ended its nuclear weapons program in 1992, it not only dismantled its weapons stockpile, the country completely shut down its entire nuclear weapons program under IAEA supervision. When Libya came clean on its weapons of mass destruction program, it turned over every scrap of illegal material and dismantled its weapons-making infrastructure. Not so here. Iran will keep the Fordow bunker "for nuclear research." It will keep its Arak reactor (albeit, modified) and all other illicit sites it developed to build an atom bomb. South Africa and Libya were nonproliferation success stories. This Iran deal will not be.

This article was originally published in the *National Interest*, July 16, 2015.

Iran is a sworn enemy of the United States. It is a revolutionary regime committed to changing the contours of the entire Middle East and destroying America's key regional ally, Israel. Iran has held American diplomats hostage, currently holds Americans—including journalists—hostage, and has killed hundreds of American servicemen and women in Lebanon, Iraq, and Afghanistan, directly or through proxies, since taking power. There is simply no evidence to support the idea that we can trust revolutionary Iran to give up its long-term goal of developing a nuclear weapon and delivery systems.

In addition to legitimizing Iran's now supposedly "peaceful" atomic program, the deal will likely lead to a nuclear arms race in the Middle East. It is hard to imagine that Sunni states such as Egypt, Turkey, and, especially, Saudi Arabia, will not immediately begin the process of procuring nuclear arms on their own or from a sympathetic third country such as Pakistan to counter Iran, which will in essence be an internationally recognized nuclear threshold state.

Further, Iran will receive tens of billions of dollars in sanctions relief. In addition to expanding its own military forces, there is no doubt that much of that money will be funneled to Iranian proxies such as Hezbollah in Lebanon, the Assad regime in Syria, Shia militias in Iraq, and Houthis rebels in Yemen—not to mention Hamas in Gaza, which Iran has supported in the past. All of these groups are at war with or threaten America's friends and allies in the region. The economics of this deal will surely increase the volatility of an already dangerous region.

President Obama claims that without this deal, the current sanctions regime covering Iran would have crumbled. This claim strains credulity. Nations that wanted to drop sanctions and trade with Iran would face the prospect of being frozen out of world banking and trade systems. Siding with Iran over America and her fifty-plus allies around the world—not to mention most Arab states, which have the same interest as America in keeping up pressure on Iran—would be an unlikely step for most nations. However, when Iran is discovered to have flouted this deal—just as it has flouted UN sanctions and the Nonproliferation Treaty over the years—it will be difficult to reimpose crippling sanctions on Tehran. The bottom line is that it's far less likely that "snap back" sanctions will ever be imposed on Iran than that the current sanctions regime would have crumbled.

It is unprecedented that President Obama is taking this major and likely damaging step in the foreign policy arena with absolutely no bipartisan support. All leading Republican candidates for president will oppose this deal with revolutionary Iran. Republican members of the House and Senate will overwhelmingly reject it. Our closest ally in the region and the Middle East's only true democracy, Israel, is dead set against the deal. The same is true for our key Arab allies. In response, the president in his press conference lumped Israeli Prime Minister Netanyahu, "the Israeli ambassador," and "the Republican leadership" into a group that must argue for a new Middle Eastern "war" as the only viable alternative to his deal with Iran's Supreme Leader. This straw-man argument that America only has a choice between the president's weak deal and "war" is so discredited as to no longer merit a serious response.

After Prime Minister Chamberlain signed the Munich Accords with the Supreme Leader of another ideological and cruel regime, Winston Churchill said in Parliament that the British people "should know that we have sustained a defeat without a war, the consequences of which will travel far with us along our road…" Sadly, his prophetic warning in 1938 appears to be applicable to us today. ■

Ukraine Votes for a Future in Europe

On Sunday night, I sat in a chilly school gym while election officials in the city of Lviv went through the tedious process of counting and reconciling paper ballots for Ukraine's parliamentary election. Millions of Ukrainians went to the polls on Sunday to elect a new Parliament, less than a year after former president and Putin puppet Viktor Yanukovych was ousted in the Maidan protests. There was no heat, because most of the gas that powers Ukraine comes from Russia and is too expensive to use this early in the season. Despite the conditions, however, I will not forget the Ukrainian people I met while observing their election.

There was a kindly grandmother running a rural polling station, who was so proud to have a foreign observer, especially an American, visit her village. She told me that the little hamlet, aptly named Velyka Volya ("Great Freedom"), was the place where a group of Ukrainian resistance fighters, in a 1946 version of Masada, committed suicide rather than surrender to the encircling Soviet troops.

An elderly man at a downtown polling station shared his story. As a medical student following the Second World War, he joined the resistance and fought the Soviets until his capture in 1951. He was shipped to a Russian gulag and survived for six years before being released, but authorities prevented him from going home. He never returned to

This article was originally published in the *National Interest*, October 29, 2014.

medical school. He was so happy to be serving as a precinct secretary in a democratic election in his native land. He pleaded with me for America to send arms and Kevlar so that Ukraine's young men would have a fighting chance against Russian regulars.

A young mother arrived at a suburban precinct. In tow was her three-year-old daughter, dressed in a white snowsuit that matched her own. The little girl clutched and waved Ukraine's blue and yellow flag and smiled the whole time that her mom underwent the formalities of casting her vote. The election was about the child. Her mom envisioned for her a future of freedom and the rule of law in the sunlit uplands of the West, not of despotism in the wintry East.

Fresh-faced kids manned the precincts. Of the seventeen precinct election committees my team visited, most had a majority of twenty-something members. Some were made up entirely of young people. The Maidan protests that claimed the lives of one hundred of their contemporaries inspired them to get involved and stop the apparatchiks from stealing another election. These young people are taking their country back. Corrupt, one-party rule has no part in their plans.

One of these young post-Maidan activists is Hanna Hopko. She is a thirty-two-year-old mom and committed Christian with a PhD in communications. Hopko has already established herself as a reformer who took on big tobacco in her effort to rid Ukraine's bars and restaurants of secondhand smoke—no easy feat in a country where cigarettes are still sold everywhere. Hopko was the number-one candidate on the Samopomich Party list. Until Sunday, Samopomich had never contested a parliamentary election. What it lacked in national election experience, it made up for with a pro-European, free-men and free-markets platform. While it appears that President Petro Poroshenko's bloc will win a narrow victory, the International Republican Institute exit poll shows Samopomich taking an unexpectedly strong third-place position. Dozens of its "outsider" candidates, led by Hopko, will now be demanding reform from inside Ukraine's Parliament.

Finally, for the first time since the Soviets occupied Ukraine in 1918, there will be no Communist Party representation in Ukraine's legislative assembly. When the exit polls were released just after 8:00 p.m., showing that the Communists were well below the 5 percent threshold for proportional representation, several Ukrainian voters pumped their fists and smiled. For them, this election was a welcome end to Communist influence over their lives.

Notwithstanding the war and the punishing economic circumstances Russia's invasion and occupation have inflicted on them, Ukrainians are happy today. They showed the world that they remain unbowed in the face of aggression and are committed to a future in the democratic West. ■

≝ | ≋

Obama's Falklands Failure

With the world's attention focused on Bashar al-Assad's violent suppression of the Syrian civilian uprising, and with the increasing likelihood of a strike by Israel to thwart Iran's relentless drive to obtain nuclear weapons, perhaps the most underreported international story is the increasingly heated dispute between Britain and Argentina in the South Atlantic Ocean. It is an unfolding issue that could say much about the way the United States handles its alliances, including those in the Asia-Pacific region.

On April 2, 1982, Argentina invaded the Falkland Islands. British Prime Minister Margaret Thatcher quickly assembled and dispatched a formidable naval task force to retake the islands, which had been in British possession since 1833. On June 14, Argentine forces surrendered to the Royal Marines. The conflict was brief but violent, with both nations losing ships and hundreds of sailors and soldiers. It was, however, a decisive victory for the United Kingdom.

As the thirtieth anniversary of the war approached, Argentina's President Cristina Kirchner vowed that her nation would reclaim Las Islas Malvinas, as the Falklands are called in Argentina. She stated that "[i]n the twenty-first century [Britain] continues to be a crude colonial power in decline." She branded British Prime Minister David Cameron

This article was originally published in the *Diplomat*, February 15, 2012.

"arrogant" and said his defense in Parliament of the right of the people of the Falklands to self-determination was an expression of "mediocrity and stupidity."

Argentina's foreign minister, Héctor Timerman, claims that Cameron's defense of the Falklands sovereignty "is perhaps the last refuge of a declining power." Argentine officials have labeled Prince William— aka Flight Lieutenant Wales, who is currently piloting a Royal Air Force rescue helicopter in the Falklands—a "conquistador."

In a diplomatic offensive, Kirchner persuaded Argentina's partners in the Mercosur trade bloc—Brazil, Paraguay, and Uruguay—to ban civilian ships flying the Falklands' flag from entering their ports. Mercosur members had previously banned British warships on Falklands duty from their ports. In December, the thirty-three-country Community of Latin American and Caribbean States unanimously backed Argentina's "legitimate rights in the sovereignty dispute" over the Falklands and South Georgia.

In response to the United Kingdom's dispatch of its newest destroyer, *HMS Dauntless*, to patrol the South Atlantic, Timerman officially complained to the United Nations Security Council that Britain had "militarized" the region. Given the timing of his complaint, just weeks before the anniversary of Argentina's invasion of the islands, it can be assumed that Timerman lacks a sense of irony. Argentina now claims that the United Kingdom is using the three thousand residents of the Falklands as a mere pretense for its desire to maintain a South Atlantic "empire." In his UN filing, Timerman noted: "It is the last ocean that is controlled by the United Kingdom—Britannia rules only the South Atlantic."

While it seems unlikely that Argentina would risk another humiliating defeat by invading the Falklands in the near term, the temptation of appealing to nationalism to mask an economic or political crisis, combined with the desire to control what appear to be significant South Atlantic oil reserves, means that another Argentine military adventure cannot be ruled out. There are four key takeaways from the current situation with implications that stretch much further than the issue at hand:

First, military weakness is provocative. Argentina ramped up its aggressive rhetoric and diplomatic efforts to reclaim the Falklands only after Prime Minister Cameron announced massive cuts to the Royal Navy and British ground forces. The decommissioning last December of the

United Kingdom's sole remaining aircraft carrier, *HMS Ark Royal*, well before its service life ended, and the sale of Britain's fifty G-9 Sea Harrier fighter jets to the US Marine Corps, seems to have emboldened the Argentines. In 1982, the Royal Navy had approximately ninety warships from which it could assemble a task force. Today it has thirty. Indeed, most experts believe that while it would be very difficult for the Argentine military to successfully invade the islands, it would be nearly impossible for the United Kingdom to retake them without an aircraft carrier in the event that Argentina was successful in overrunning Britain's key air base at Mount Pleasant.

There's a clear analogy between Argentina's response to Britain's defense cuts and what we can expect in the South China Sea and Persian Gulf from China and Iran, respectively, as massive sequestration cuts threaten to decimate the United States military. Indeed, the Obama administration announced this week that the US Navy will decommission seven Ticonderoga-class cruisers and two amphibious warships in 2012 alone. There's no doubt that Beijing, Tehran, and even Moscow are watching the slashing of the US defense budget with the same attention that Buenos Aires is paying to the decline of the Royal Navy.

Second, the Obama administration has made the United States an unreliable ally for our closest friends. Britain has been a stalwart ally of the United States in both Iraq and Afghanistan, notwithstanding the tremendous domestic political pressure on Labour and Conservative governments not to participate in those unpopular wars. However, in 2010, Secretary of State Hillary Clinton called for talks over the dispute and even appeared to side with Argentina during a press conference with President Kirchner in Buenos Aires. Last month, as the current situation developed, rather than send a clear message to Argentina that the United States supported its longtime ally, a State Department spokesman demurred: "[t]his is a bilateral issue that needs to be worked out directly between the governments of Argentina and the United Kingdom....We recognize de facto United Kingdom administration of the islands, but take no position regarding sovereignty." Nile Gardiner, the *Telegraph*'s Washington correspondent, wrote in response that the "Obama administration knife[d] Britain in the back again over the Falklands."

The shabby treatment meted out to America's "special relationship" partner in this instance cannot be seen as a surprise. It is in line with the administration's treatment of Israel and Prime Minister Benjamin Netanyahu (at least prior to Bob Turner winning Anthony Weiner's Congressional seat in New York). Poland and the Czech Republic suffered similar slights after the administration unilaterally cancelled ABM sites in those countries as part of its naïve—and so far unsuccessful—attempt to "reset" relations with Russia. And there has been much criticism of the administration for failing to provide Taiwan with the latest F-16 fighters that it has long requested to defend itself against a potential attack by China. There is no doubt that American allies such as Israel, Colombia, Georgia, Taiwan, the Gulf States, and the Baltics, all of which live in dangerous neighborhoods, are watching the United States' response to the Falklands row with concern.

Third, failing to promote the rule of law, democracy, and self-determination in the Falklands will damage the United States' ability to promote those goals in other nations. The 3,200 residents of the Falklands have been there for over 175 years. They descend from people who have inhabited the islands for far longer than many Argentines have inhabited their own country. They are, apparently without exception, in favor of maintaining their local parliamentary government and association with Britain. There are no Argentines on the islands and there are no "displaced" refugees in Argentina seeking a "right of return." The current diplomatic crisis follows the nationalistic playbook that President Kirchner borrowed from the former military junta and that is promoted by her mentor in Caracas. The fact that there are large oil reserves off the Falklands is also fueling Argentine territorial ambitions as its government would love to get control of such resources.

Unfortunately, Falklanders should expect little support from the United Nations for their rights in the face of any Argentine aggression. The deaf ears of the international community to the pleas of Syrian civilian protestors in Horns, Zimbabwean farmers of British descent, Iranian democracy advocates, or Chinese dissidents should steel them for their future should Argentina seek to take over their islands. Thus, while it may be inconvenient for the United States to assist Britain in ensuring the rights of a small number of farmers and fishermen on distant shores, its failure to do so will undermine American moral authority to protect victims of aggression elsewhere. For example, the complex web of territorial claims in the South China Sea requires that no party try to unilaterally impose its will on smaller neighbors. The question is what sort of precedent the South Atlantic crisis sets for this similarly tense dispute in the Pacific.

Fourth, Argentina's efforts to damage the economy of the Falklands will backfire. By banning ships flying the Falklands flag from its ports and encouraging its trading partners to do the same, Argentina is denying its people and its neighbors the benefits that could accrue from the burgeoning oil exploration boom in the South Atlantic and the shore-based support services that will follow. Additionally, tourism in the Falklands and Antarctic region is a growing business that could benefit Argentina as well as the islands. Further, Argentine instructions to its commercial fishing fleet to over-fish the Illex squid population as the schools migrate from the South American coast to the South Atlantic could truly harm the species while having minimal impact on Falklands' fishing license revenue.

Still, it's unlikely that the negative economic effects of Argentina's Falklands embargo campaign will dissuade President Kirchner from continuing down this path. During her presidency and that of her late husband, the rule of law and market principles have been weakened dramatically, as was evidenced by the government's seizure in 2008 of nearly $30 billion in private pension funds. Based on this record, it is hard to believe that any argument against Falklands aggression that appeals to Argentina's economic self-interest would be well received by the Argentine government.

Whatever the outcome of the current crisis over the Falklands, the Obama administration's failure to back America's key ally, coupled with its policy of significantly cutting American defenses, sends the wrong message that will be heard far beyond the waters of the South Atlantic. ∎

Welcome to the UNGA

M y thirteen-year-old son, who is far more interested in sports than politics, walked into the family room yesterday and said: "Dad, I saw on the news that the thing is starting when all the dictators come to America and give speeches about how bad we are." His statement is one of the better descriptions of the United Nations General Assembly that I have ever heard.

For those who do not regularly follow the opening of the UN, here are some things you can expect to see this week.

Iranian President Mohammad Ahmadinejad will claim that there are no human rights abuses in Iran (stoning is merely an ancient method of execution that the United States is exaggerating to create propaganda against Iran), that the American hikers are spies, that Iran is developing nuclear power for peaceful purposes, and that he is definitely not anti-Semitic, all of which he told Christiane Amanpour on her Sunday program.

The one true thing he will say is that UN sanctions against Iran are "meaningless." They are. He dismissed them as a "joke" to Amanpour. He is right. They will not delay or stop Iran's march to obtaining a nuclear bomb. He may renew his call for "Israel to be wiped off the map." If he does not, the press will hail the omission as a sign of Iranian moderation.

This article was originally published in the *Daily Caller*, September 21, 2010.

Israel will be castigated in speeches for everything from the fact it continues to build homes for its citizens in its own capital to its navy's interception of the blockade-running "humanitarian" ships of the Gaza flotilla. Sadly, it will not be just the dictators who slam Israel; far too many Western democracies will also bash Israel to curry favor with the assembly.

Few, if any, delegates will mention the thousands of Hamas rockets that have poured down on the Jewish state since its unilateral withdrawal from Gaza. Nor will anyone point out the irony that fellow UN member states have argued that Israel, a full member of the General Assembly, should cease to exist as a nation.

Over the next several days, American, Japanese, and European tax-payers will be badgered into pledging more money for the world's poor. The UN Secretary-General Ban Ki-moon has already set up the "ask" by claiming in his report on the Millennium Summit goals this summer that "improvements in the lives of the poor have been unacceptably slow, and some hard-won gains are being eroded by the climate, food, and economic crises."

Of course, China, the world's second-largest economy, with trillions in foreign reserves, will be asked for little and will volunteer even less. No one will complain. It would not matter if they did. The Chinese look out for their national interests only and are not swayed by UN guilt trips.

Further, little mention will be made of the fact that most of the world's poor live in countries with abundant natural resources that are squandered daily by thugs and strongmen. These dictators are more interested in lining their pockets, pursuing failed ideologies, undermining their democratic neighbors, or abusing the human rights of opposition parties than they are in alleviating the poverty of their people.

Again, there will be few complaints. To point out such unpleasant facts at the UN would be undiplomatic because such "leaders" will all be present in the assembly hall. A diplomat who scolds might bump into one of the tyrants at the shrimp platter, which could make the reception following the day's session a bit awkward.

President Obama will be on hand to assure the delegates that America is no longer exceptional in international affairs. He will say something along the lines of his maiden speech last year: "In an era when our destiny is shared, power is no longer a zero-sum game. No one nation can or should try to control another nation. No world order that elevates one nation or group of people over another will succeed. No balance of power among nations will hold."

The dictators will be pleased to hear this message but will not give him anything in return. The president will smile broadly, talk about his new era of engagement with the UN, and head home.

Those who believe that something useful might actually get done at the General Assembly will not see any of the following:

The assembly will not condemn North Korea for its unprovoked submarine attack on the *Cheonan*, in which forty-six South Korean sailors were killed.

The assembly will not put teeth into its sanctions against Iran for ignoring the IAEA or its obligations under the Nonproliferation Treaty.

Cuba will not be cited for the dreadful conditions in which its political prisoners are held. As the elected vice-chair of the UN's Human Rights Commission, Cuba is immune from such a reprimand.

The UN will do nothing for the suffering people of Burma, Iran, or North Korea, and Chavez will continue his brutal conversion of Venezuela into his own personal Bolivarian fiefdom without a peep from the assembled great and good.

The United States will not push for UN reform to root out fraud, waste, and abuse that divert American tax dollars from the truly needy to who-knows-where.

In about a week's time, after they have told the United States how bad we are, demanded more money from donor countries, and finished their Secret Service-escorted shopping trips on Fifth Avenue, the dictators will go home. That is good news for us—and bad news for their countries. ∎

SECTION 2

≡ | ≋

A Hollow Force?

≋ | ≋

End Sequestration Now
National Defense Panel is Right (And So Was Romney)

As American warplanes return to Iraq to bomb ISIS targets today, it is clear that it has not been a good year for freedom. Islamists, bent on genocide against religious minorities, established a caliphate in Iraq and Syria. They now menace Lebanon and Kurdistan.

Vladimir Putin invaded and annexed Crimea—the first territorial conquest by force in Europe since World War II. Ukraine remains in peril. The Baltics, Georgia, and Moldova wonder if their turn is next. China claims almost the entire South China Sea and plans to dot the Paracel and Spratly Islands with airstrips, lighthouses, and oil rigs. In the East China Sea, Beijing is in a dangerous standoff with Japan as it seeks to wrest the Senkaku Islands away from Tokyo.

Hamas launched a rocket and terror tunnel war on Israel and gained sympathy by using human shields to thwart Israel's defense.

Salafist jihadis have almost overrun Libya and remain a threat in Mali. Boko Haram kidnaps, murders, and maims in Nigeria.

Nuclear North Korea lurks in the background and Iran gets closer to breakout each day that it strings the West along in negotiations over its enrichment program. Madeleine Albright calls the world "a mess." John Bolton says we are "descending into chaos."

This article was originally published on *FoxNews.com*, October 4, 2013.

It is, therefore, not surprising that the nonpartisan National Defense Panel (NDP), in its independent report on the Pentagon's 2014 Quadrennial Defense Review stated, "in the current threat environment, America could plausibly be called upon to deter or fight in any number of regions in overlapping time frames: on the Korean peninsula, in the East or South China Sea, South Asia, in the Middle East, the Trans-Sahel, Sub-Saharan Africa, in Europe, and possibly elsewhere."

Thus, the NDP's finding that the United States "is facing major readiness shortfalls" is troubling. The NDP notes we are on the path to "a hollow force that loses its best people, underfunds procurement, and shortchanges innovation." According to the panel, that "each service is experiencing degradations in so many areas at once is especially troubling at a time of growing security challenges."

NDP member and former Missouri senator Jim Talent called the unanimous report "a stunning rebuke of the government's defense policies over the last three years." It is worth comparing the NDP Report to Mitt Romney's 2012 national security white paper, *An American Century.*

Romney wrote then: "Instead of rebuilding our strength, President Obama has put us on course toward a 'hollow' force [while] American troops are in combat in Afghanistan, facing dangers in Iraq, and fighting the remnants of al-Qaeda worldwide."

The NDP calls for a larger Navy and Air Force to face our current threats: "The Navy, which bears the largest burden of forward-presence missions, is on a budgetary path to 260 ships or less. We believe the fleet-size requirement to be...323 ships [to] 346 ships...and an even larger fleet may be necessary if the risk of conflict in the Western Pacific increases.... The Air Force now fields the smallest and oldest force of combat aircraft in its history yet needs a global surveillance and strike force able to rapidly deploy to theaters of operation to deter, defeat, or punish multiple aggressors simultaneously."

Romney said the same two years ago: "The Navy has only 284 ships today, the lowest level since 1916. Given current trends, the number will decline...Our naval planners indicate we need 328 ships to fulfill the Navy's role of global presence and power projection in defense of American security." With respect to airpower, he observed, "our Air Force, which had 82 fighter squadrons at the end of the Cold War, has been reduced to 39 today."

In light of this hollow force crisis, the NDP concludes: "Congress and the President should repeal the Budget Control Act immediately," as repealing sequestration "is the minimum required to reverse course and set the military on a more stable footing."

The administration insisted on sequestration. It assumed that Republicans, whose constituents they believed to be more committed to defense than their Democratic base, would agree to domestic spending increases in order to avoid the hollow force crisis into which we are now plunging.

Given the deteriorating worldwide situation, the administration can no longer afford to use America's military as a bargaining chip to ratchet up domestic spending. For an administration intent on avoiding American boots on the ground overseas, the immediate repeal of sequestration is its best play.

Such a move will signal to friend and foe alike that American power is rebounding and, in turn, will strengthen the hands of American diplomats seeking to resolve the plethora of crises facing the world. As the NDP explains, "the effectiveness of America's other tools for global engagement is critically dependent upon the perceived strength and presence of America's hard power as well as our resolve to use that power when necessary." ■

⇒ | ⇐

The Dangers of Defense Sequestration

Former Secretary of State Madeleine Albright recently called the world "a mess." With a resurgent Russia chasing czarist glory through invasions and occupations of Ukraine, Georgia, and Moldova, the cruel Islamic State establishing itself as a power in Mesopotamia, soon-to-be-nuclear Iran building a Shia proxy arc from Hezbollah-controlled Lebanon on the Mediterranean through Syria and Iraq to Yemen on the Arabian Peninsula, and China scooping up islands throughout the South China Sea, Albright's comment is an understatement.

It is at precisely this time, perhaps the most dangerous point in world history since 1938, that the Obama administration is downsizing America's defenses through astonishing budget cuts compounded by defense "sequestration." Mackenzie Eaglen, the American Enterprise Institute's highly respected defense analyst, concludes the "drawdown of the last six years has been unlike any other in modern times. It is modest in percentage and dollar terms, but steeper in practical effect and reduced output. What is essentially a 20 percent cut in spending will feel more like double when it is over." These cuts imperil American security and put our servicemen and women at risk.

America's defense drawdown erodes military readiness and risks creating a "hollow force" not seen since the post-Vietnam days of the

---

This article was originally published in the *Daily Journal*, November 18, 2014.

Carter administration. Six of the Navy's fleet of ten aircraft carriers are currently in dock undergoing some type of significant maintenance. Chief of Naval Operations Admiral Jonathan Greenert said that due to sequestration, "we...stopped work on some of the projects in the shipyards: the *Vinson* we slowed down dramatically, the *Reagan*, and the *George H. W. Bush*" were also impacted. Down from fifteen carriers during the Reagan years, the Navy simply cannot conduct its required missions under such circumstances for much longer.

Greenert noted that deployments, which used to last six months, now keep our sailors at sea for nine months or more. "That's not sustainable," he stated, and there is no relief in sight. The long deployments and heavy operational pace have taken their toll not only on sailor morale, but also on the carriers and their escorts themselves. Excess wear and tear caused the *USS Lincoln*'s catapult water break to become so worn that maintenance folks had never seen such damage. The *USS Roosevelt* has problems with its arresting gear water cooler. Damage to the *USS Eisenhower*'s shafts, rudders, and distilling unit will keep it in maintenance well into 2015. Sequestration will force the Navy to mothball half the cruiser fleet, the warships that ride shotgun for the carriers.

The Navy's elite Top Gun school, where aviators train in aerial combat tactics, is practically grounded due to lack of serviceable planes. F/A-18 Hornet fighter squadrons often have only two or three fighters that are flyable. Scores of Hornets await maintenance because spare parts are not available or must be cannibalized from other planes. Boeing and the Navy lack engineers to inspect and maintain the versions of the fighter. Idled aircraft mean idled pilots, who are deprived of their ability to train prior to deployment to conflict zones.

Readiness is not just a Navy problem. Air Force Chief of Staff General Mark Welsh said his "airplanes are falling apart...They're just flat too old." In 2007, F-15 fighters were grounded during high tempo operations in Iraq and Afghanistan due to cracks in their canopies. The same thing happened to F-16D fighters last month.

In a recent speech, Army General John Campbell warned: "In the event of a crisis, we'll deploy units at a significantly lower readiness level but our soldiers are adaptive and agile, and over time, they will accomplish their mission. But their success will come with a greater cost of higher casualties." Newly retired Marine Corps Commandant General

James Amos told Congress essentially the same thing: "The primary concern with out-of-balance readiness of our non-deployed operating forces is an increased risk in the timely response to unexpected crisis or large-scale contingencies."

The 2014 bipartisan panel headed by former Clinton administration Secretary of Defense William Perry tasked with reviewing the Pentagon's budget planning came to the following conclusion: "Today the [Department of Defense] is facing major readiness shortfalls that will, absent a decisive reversal of course, create the possibility of a hollow force that loses its best people, underfunds procurement, and shortchanges innovation. The fact that each service is experiencing degradations in so many areas at once is especially troubling at a time of growing security challenges." Former Senator Jim Talent, a member of the panel, called its unanimous report "a stunning rebuke of the government's defense policies over the last three years."

It appears that the administration finally is beginning to understand the hollow force crisis. Deputy Defense Secretary Robert Work told a Washington think tank last week that "it would be unconscionable to send American troops into a fight where they are not adequately trained and equipped." The White House insisted on defense sequestration during the 2012 budget showdown to give itself a future chit to trade for increased domestic spending. But defense sequestration will result in a hollow force that undermines American security and subjects our soldiers, sailors, airmen, Marines, and Coast Guardsmen to unnecessary risk. America and those who defend her deserve better than to be used for such political bargaining, especially in light of the "mess" the world faces. Ending defense sequestration should be the first item on the agenda for the president and new Congress in January. ■

We Need a Militarily Strong, Morally Confident America
It's Time for Smart Power

The national security debate in Washington is a muddled affair. Israeli Prime Minister Netanyahu warned us Tuesday at the UN that conciliatory gestures from an Iranian regime bent on nuclear domination of the Middle East are a ruse. But in Washington, no one seems to be listening—or preparing for the dangerous new world Netanyahu outlined.

President Obama continues to "lead from behind," first following the French and now the Russians in ad hoc decision making on a crisis-by-crisis basis.

Republican Senators John McCain and Lindsey Graham's reflexive solution to any situation is apparently to call for the imposition of a no-fly zone.

But the no-fly zone option is becoming a more complicated proposition for our armed forces as "Tea Party" Republicans join "San Francisco" Democrats in embracing sequestration, which is literally decimating the American military and could sideline four carrier battle groups.

Dennis Kucinich-led progressives are allied with Ron Paul-led libertarians in advocating a new era of American isolationism, hoping that by withdrawing from the world, the world's problems will stop at our shores.

Missing in the debate are vocal advocates of the formerly bipartisan postwar consensus that a militarily strong and morally confident

This article was originally published in the *Diplomat*, October 4, 2013.

America, actively engaged with its allies in the world, is a force for peace and good.

Ronald Reagan called the approach "peace through strength." Now into the void steps former Bush administration State Department official, Christian Whiton, with his book, *Smart Power: Between Diplomacy and War*.

Whiton makes the case for a robust foreign policy that pursues the nation's interests using the full spectrum of the foreign policy tools in America's toolbox. He argues that there is a fertile "smart power" middle ground between diplomacy and war, which can be cultivated to harvest American national interests. He points to American postwar success in stopping the spread of communism in Western Europe as the high point for the use of smart power.

Starting in 1948, the United States and its allies fought the Soviet Union and its proxies intellectually (e.g., broadcasting Radio Free Europe), economically (implementing the Marshall Plan), overtly (ending the post-World War II military drawdown), and covertly (providing direct clandestine aide to anticommunist parties).

Ronald Reagan rejoined the fight and further enhanced the West's position when he deployed new classes of American nuclear weapons (Pershing II missiles and cruise missiles) to Europe in 1983 to counter the Red Army's numerically superior armored and infantry divisions. He also provided covert aid to freedom fighters in Central America and Africa.

Shortly thereafter, occupied Eastern Europe was free and the Soviet Union had disintegrated—not as a result of war but through the systematic application of American smart power.

Fast-forward to today.

Consider the United States' hasty withdrawal from Iraq, which is on the verge of renewed sectarian chaos, its lack of a clear exit plan in Afghanistan, its management of the fiascos in Libya, Egypt, and Syria, and the lack of Western will to defend Georgia, where the Brezhnev Doctrine seems to have been resurrected by Russia. Add to this the failure to respond meaningfully to Chinese assertiveness in the Pacific, and the West's inability to stop Iran's relentless march toward a nuclear bomb—a game changer in the Middle East. Whiton concludes that America lacks both global and regional smart power strategies to advance its interests.

Whiton's proposed solution to America's smart power deficiency is also the shortcoming in his otherwise well-reasoned book. Having lost confidence in the State Department and CIA bureaucracies, he advocates the creation of a new government agency that would have the communications tasking of the former US Information Agency and the political warfare and intelligence collection capabilities of the World War Two Office of Strategic Services.

Rather than create another bureaucracy in a foreign-policy and national-security arena that is already an alphabet soup, the conservative approach would be to bring strong leadership to bear in refocusing State, Defense, the CIA, and their sister departments on their roles in implementing US smart power initiatives.

Ironically, the country that seems to be best employing the type of smart power and its subcomponent, political warfare, advocated by Whiton, is the looming adversary that concerns him most—China.

Whiton argues it is China "that wages relentless cyberwar on the United States, that is building a navy to exclude the United States from the Western Pacific, that trades unfairly, and that systematically steals American technology and intellectual property to improve its military and damage America's economy." Further, Whiton claims, even Pentagon officials are unwilling to criticize China's "peaceful rise" for fear of being accused of having a "Cold War mindset," a cleverly coined phrase deployed by the Chinese government.

Accordingly, Whiton should not be surprised if the first country to seek translation rights for his book is China. There may be more interest in Beijing in his smart power theories and strategies today than there is in Washington.

From China to Iran and across the Middle East the world is becoming more dangerous for America and its allies. Rather than ignore the warning provided this week by Prime Minister Netanyahu at the UN, we should get smarter about confronting our adversaries. ∎

SECTION 3

⇉ | ⇇

To Rule the Waves

⇛ | ⇚

The Navy's Hidden Crisis
It's Too Small—and Getting Smaller

Not many Americans understand how many Army divisions we have, the percentage breakdown of the Air Force's fighter/bomber mix, or the three "triad" legs of our strategic nuclear force. But just about everyone understands the Navy's "ship count" and what it means for a president to send a carrier battle group into a crisis zone. And so, amid a more complicated and complex discussion this week over the sequestration's impact, it didn't go unnoticed Wednesday when Ashton Carter, President Obama's defense secretary nominee, told Congress that the aircraft carrier fleet would likely continue to shrink.

It was only the latest revelation, though, about how deeply and quickly the Navy's ambitions are shrinking—even in an age when our adversaries are growing their own navies in oceans around the world. Ever since Theodore Roosevelt's "Great White Fleet," the US Navy has been how the country's leaders have projected power on the world stage—but it's now clear from years of cutbacks, sequestration, and an aging fleet that we're going to be doing less of that power projection in the years ahead.

What's not clear, though, is that "less" is the right answer—a topic that's going to be front and center in the debates over the nation's military as we enter the 2016 presidential race. There will be a dozen voices on the GOP side alone—each struggling to connect with their own "peace

This article was originally published in *Politico Magazine*, February 5, 2015.

through strength" message, grabbing the mantle of Ronald Reagan in some capacity or another. When talk in the debates and on the campaign trail turns to defense and national security issues, candidates will need a shorthand message to communicate seriousness on the subject. Many candidates struggle to communicate their clear and steady commitment to American exceptionalism and a strong defense without losing audiences by diving too deep into defense minutia and acronyms. After having been involved in the last three presidential campaigns, I can say with certainty that the shortcut to connecting with voters on national security is via a discussion of the strength of the United States Navy. The American voter knows that we cannot protect the seas and our interests overseas unless we have ships that can fight and deliver Marines and carrier-based fighter jets to the world's hot spots.

Here's the starting point for that discussion: we have a crisis in the fleet, and serious contenders on both sides of 2016 should have a plan for fixing it—and fast. Today, at 284 warships, the United States Navy's fleet is the smallest since World War I. But even that number probably overstates the Navy's true capability: the Pentagon recently changed the rules by which it counts active warships and if you apply the traditional and more stringent method, the Navy has but 274 warships.

Due to budget cuts and the follow-on threat of sequestration, the carrier fleet will likely shrink from the Congressionally mandated eleven to ten—or even lower. *Politico* reported that Carter further refused to agree to preserve the Navy's fleet at a specific level, dodging the question by maintaining that "ship count is only one metric...to evaluate fleet effectiveness."

The Obama administration's failure to stem the Navy's decline comes amid recent reports that China's PLA Navy will surpass the US Navy in the total number of warships by 2020—a troubling imbalance since the Chinese navy is concentrated heavily in the South China Sea, whereas ours is spread around the entire globe. Russia has also embarked on a naval modernization program focusing on new submarines and destroyers. It is also expanding or building new naval bases in the Arctic, Pacific, and Black Sea. Russia and China have both invested heavily in asymmetrical anti-access/area denial (A2/AD) capabilities to deter the United States Navy from approaching waters near their shores. As the Navy gets smaller, the world's oceans are becoming more dangerous.

The Secretary of the Navy's "Report to Congress on the Annual Long-Range Plan for Construction of Naval Vessels for FY2015" documented a requirement of 306 ships for the Navy based on the Pentagon's 2012 Force Structure Analysis. That number is certainly too low and—as the Congressional Budget Office has found—is at any rate unachievable under the current budget trend lines. No one in Washington would bet his own money that the Navy will grow in the decades ahead. In fact, given current budgetary trends, the Navy will shrink to around 240–250 ships, and America will no longer be the global naval power it is today.

It is important to remember that at any given time, the Navy can only keep about one-third of its ships at sea; ships have to be maintained, and crews have to train and rest. The Obama administration has stated that it needs sixty-seven ships on station in the Western Pacific. So if the Navy were sustained at three hundred ships, and if the requirements for the Western Pacific were met, the Navy would have thirty-three ships available to carry out its missions in the rest of the world at any given time.

The bipartisan National Defense Panel's report on the 2014 Quadrennial Defense Review recommended a Navy of between 323 and 346 ships and warned that if China's power and provocations continue to grow—and there is no sign whatsoever they won't—the Navy would need to be even larger.

Given Russia's invasion and occupation of the Crimea, proxy war in Eastern Ukraine and saber-rattling in the Baltic region, rising tensions between China and its neighbors in the East and South China Sea, and increasing demand for sea-based anti-ballistic missile defense around the world, especially as Iran and North Korea ramp up their ICBM programs, the Navy's 2012 analysis has been overtaken by events and the number of ships it deems necessary to fulfill its mission is certainly too low. In light of growing tension across the world's oceans and seas, this bipartisan recommendation of between 323 and 346 ships should be considered a floor rather than a ceiling.

Yet under the Navy's current plan, the ship count will not reach 306 until 2022 and will never rise above 316 ships. Further, independent analysts from Congressional Budget Office and Congressional Research Service believe that current shipbuilding funding, even assuming that sequestration is reversed, is entirely inadequate to execute the Navy's stated 306-ship plan. The Secretary of the Navy's own report concedes that the current funding levels for shipbuilding are not adequate to fund both the shipbuilding plan and to replace the Ohio-class ballistic missile submarines. The Ohio-class submarines account for one-third of America's nuclear triad and are due to retire in the 2025–2035 time-frame. The replacement of the least vulnerable leg of the nuclear triad is a national priority and, thus, simply must be funded.

The administration that will take office in January 2017 regrettably has few tools left to address both the short- and long-term issues impact-ing fleet size. For many decades, the Navy maintained a large number of inactive ships which received caretaker maintenance and were, therefore, available to be placed back into service relatively quickly should the need arise. Since 1997, however, the number of inactive ships maintained by the Navy has dropped from over two hundred to fewer than fifty. The rate at which the reserve fleet is being wiped out has hastened under the Obama administration.

Just recently, all six remaining US-owned ships of a class of modern minesweepers—the Osprey-class coastal minehunters (MHC 51)—were scrapped. Further, there are current plans to scrap two Avenger-class mine countermeasures ships (MCM 1), which are out of service but could quickly be deployed to the Persian Gulf and East China Sea. These moves are particularly shortsighted since the recently announced "upgunned" version of the Littoral Combat Ship will no longer support a mine coun-termeasures mission. Together with anti-ship ballistic (ASBM) and cruise missiles (ASCM) and quiet submarines, maritime mines are a key asym-metrical tool that can be used by American adversaries—Iran used them extensively in the 1980s in the Persian Gulf. The unnecessary loss of the Osprey and Avenger platforms is, thus, particularly troubling.

Even as the reserve fleet is lost, following defense budget cuts and defense contractor consolidation, America has precious few shipyards capable of building major warships. The vendor base for critical ship components in several key cases has only one or two potential suppliers, which are small and cannot readily scale up to provide shipyards with more than the currently planned number of components. With dedicated and responsible action by the new administration and this Congress, it may still be possible to reverse what is quickly becoming irreparable damage to the fleet.

First, the eleven-carrier commitment must be maintained and funded by Congress even in the face of current the administration's hostility to a fleet of that size. Carriers still matter. No navy in the world can put to sea a ship comparable to the 100,000-ton-displacement American CVNs, which are powered by two nuclear reactors, carry up to eighty-five aircraft, and are crewed by over five thousand sailors and aviators when their air wings are embarked.

It is for this reason that in a crisis, the first question asked by an American president is, "Where are the carriers?" It is also the reason that the Philippines, our ally, recently welcomed the *USS Stennis* and its escorts into the neighborhood as a counterweight to the region's assertive superpower, China. It is the reason our commanders in Afghanistan and Iraq can send soldiers and Marines into desolate and hostile environments. They rely on fighters launched from the carrier decks to deliver ordnance, on demand, to support the ground troops' missions. These carrier-based aircraft do not require bases in the war zone or in nearby, and often fickle, allied nations. And it is why China, which has been developing anti-access and area-denial strategies to deter the United States from sending its carriers into the Western Pacific, is building a fleet of five carriers.

Second, inactive ships, and ships facing near-term decommissioning that still offer the Navy meaningful war-fighting capability, should immediately be prohibited by Congress from being scrapped or sold until the next administration takes office. There are currently ten Oliver Hazzard Perry-class frigates, thirteen Los Angeles-class submarines, and one amphibious assault ship due to be decommissioned and either sold or scrapped in the next five years. Additionally, there are three Denver-class dock landing ships currently in the inactive fleet that could be reactivated to provide immediate amphibious capability. While all twenty-seven of these ships are relatively old, they could fill a capability gap until an increased number of new warships can be built. In all but a few cases, they still outclass any ship they would confront in a conflict. With these twenty-seven ships, and maintaining current building plans, the Navy would reach 306 warships by 2017 and could exceed 326 ships in 2019.

The Navy's recently announced concept of "distributed lethality," whereby it will enable everything that floats to fight by adding or upgrading weapons systems on its ships, is particularly suited to these older platforms. For example, it would be very useful to extend the amphibious carrier *USS Peleliu*'s life for ten years so that the ship remains available to deploy marines in a contingency. Additionally, using the ship's massive flight deck and hangers as a platform to test and deploy VSTOL and VTOL aircraft and UAVs, such as the Fire Scout, as well as new lasers and rail guns, could create a powerful surface combatant.

Turkey has already taken such an approach with the Perry-class frigates it purchased from the United States. Turkey's frigates, now the G-Class, have been kitted with advanced radars and an eight-cell MK 41 Vertical Launching System. The updated ships possess the ability to employ several variants of the long-range surface-to-air Standard Missiles, the short-range surface-to-air Evolved Sea Sparrow Missiles, and the RGM-84 Harpoon anti-ship missiles. These frigates are now among the most lethal ships in the Mediterranean. Australia executed a similar upgrade to four of its frigates. There is no reason the United States cannot match Turkey and Australia in upgrading its remaining Perry-class frigates.

The important gain in ship count as outlined above would be temporary; it is unlikely those twenty-seven ships would have any more than ten to fifteen years of additional useful service life, although ship life extension programs are becoming more effective and sophisticated. Buying time with these ships, however, would allow the Navy to build the new warships it requires to protect the global commons for the remainder of this century.

Third, over the long term, to maintain a fleet of 326 or more cutting-edge warships requires an increase in the rate of shipbuilding. Prompt action is a must as building modern warships involves a long lead time. Virginia-class submarines and Arleigh Burke-class destroyers take roughly four years to build. Both of these ship classes are built at two different yards; the current Navy plan calls for one ship per year per yard over the next several years. Fortunately, even with the current diminished industrial base, there exists sufficient capacity to increase this build rate to two ships per yard per year for both classes.

The Virginia-class submarine is perhaps the best antidote to A2/AD capabilities. With their wide variety of weapons, including underwater robots, the Virginias can stealthily dominate in even the most inhospitable coastal environments. Arleigh Burke-class destroyers with their

Aegis combat suite and vertical launch systems can defend carriers and amphibs in an asymmetrical environment as well as provide offensive punch. While these high-tech platforms are expensive, they are critical to maintaining America's edge against potential adversaries, whether they seek to deny access throughout the Western Pacific, the Persian Gulf, or even the Mediterranean Sea.

Since the Navy has been building submarines and destroyers at a lower rate for the past decade, the nation's main challenge will be rebuilding the human capital at these four shipyards. Provided a long-term stable shipbuilding plan is approved and funded, defense contractors should be able to make the required investment to expand their workforce. If production increased starting in fiscal year 2017, by 2024 there would be an additional ten to twelve major warships over the current plan, with additional ships every year thereafter to replace those ships reactivated to fill the current gap as they reach the end of their extended service life.

The recapitalization of the Navy's fleet on the foregoing basis would yield an additional sixteen commissioned warships by 2024, bringing the projected total fleet to 329 ships by the time the next president is likely to leave office. Maintaining this shipbuilding rate would then allow for the responsible retirement of the twenty-seven ships reactivated to fill our current fleet size gap. Such an undertaking will be neither inexpensive nor easy. It is not, however, dissimilar to the CBO's recommendation for the Navy. The additional budget required for such a program would be approximately $10 billion dollars per year with new funds appropriated for the operations and manpower accounts to crew and deploy the ships. While significant, this amount can surely be funded out of a total federal budget of $3.8 trillion.

It is hard for anyone born after 1945 to imagine a world where the oceans—the global commons—are not open for trade and commerce or where freedom of navigation is imperiled. The benefits to this country and the international community of the Pax Americana that has existed at sea for so long are derived from a robust American Navy. If America does not immediately reverse the decline of its fleet, free trade, commerce, and navigation will be at serious risk—as will be the very security of our nation. Supporting the US Navy will be a winning message for any candidate in 2016.

After all, it's a message that can resonate with just about any voter. ∎

Obama Failed to Mention Loss of Aircraft Carrier from Navy Fleet

When it comes to the importance of maintaining a strong United States Navy, Governor Romney was right and President Obama was wrong.

"We have fewer ships than we did in 1916. Well, governor, we also have fewer horses and bayonets, because the nature of our military's changed. We have these things called aircraft carriers, where planes land on them." That unfortunate quip was, of course, made by President Obama at the debate on foreign policy at Lynn University earlier this month.

What the President failed to mention is that in December of this year, we'll have one less of those "things called aircraft carriers" when the *USS Enterprise* is retired.

In 2013, the US Navy will have fewer carriers—ten—than the Congressionally mandated fleet. Assuming that sequestration and additional Obama defense cuts are implemented, defense experts believe that it is likely that the carrier fleet will shrink further still.

One defense contractor who manages the building of new carriers told *Businessweek* that the cuts are an "end-of-earth scenario."

This article was originally published on *Newsmax.com*, October 30, 2012.

Of those ten carriers still in the fleet, using today's deployments as a model, just four would be at sea at any given time. Only one—the *USS George Washington*—would be forward deployed in Asia.

The other three would likely be found in the Persian Gulf, Arabian Sea (supporting US forces in Afghanistan), and involved in training exercises.

Of the remaining six carriers, two would be in post-deployment status in their home ports and four would be in short-, medium-, or long-term maintenance and unavailable during a crisis.

As Governor Romney correctly pointed out in the debate, the US Navy is the smallest it has been since World War I, standing some twenty-eight warships below the minimum 313 warships that the Navy has said are necessary to fulfill its global missions.

At the same time, China has embarked on a massive buildup of its People's Liberation Army Navy and Vladimir Putin has announced that Russia will invest hundreds of billions of petro-dollars into expanding the Russian fleet.

The centerpiece of China's naval modernization is a new fleet of aircraft carriers. China launched its first carrier in September—the *Liaoning*. That ship began touch-and-go flight training this month with China's J-15 Flying Shark fighter.

The *Liaoning*, a totally refurbished ex-Soviet Kuznetsov-class ship, is just the start for China. Several weeks ago at a major maritime security conference in Canada, a senior Chinese official told attendees that China planned on building three indigenous "big" carriers and that they would be "nuclear." He also attempted to soothe any Western concerns by claiming that China's carriers would be "friendly" to America.

While it may take a decade or more for China to reach these goals, and while the United States may temporarily increase its carrier force when the new Ford-class carriers start joining the fleet (barring sequestration style cuts), it is clear that there will soon be a new naval aviation balance in the Pacific that is not entirely good for the US Navy.

Because America's obligations are global, at any given time it is likely that only one American carrier would be at sea in the Asia-Pacific region. China's primary maritime goals, on the other hand, are regional: it seeks to incorporate large swaths of the East and South China Seas into its territorial waters. With four carriers in its fleet, it will likely have two carriers at sea in the Asia-Pacific region.

The US Navy has ensured our nation's prosperity and contributed to the rise of world economic growth for the better part of a century by maintaining the freedom of the seas—the global commons. When a crisis occurs, the American president's first question is, and will be for many years to come, "where are the carriers?" Yet by its own analysis, the US Navy does not have sufficient ships to carry out its missions—and the carrier fleet is getting smaller.

Indeed, in a future contingency, the US Navy might even be outnumbered in a particular theater. Joking that having fewer American warships in the water to keep the sea lanes open is the equivalent to having fewer horse-mounted cavalry brigades sadly demonstrates a lack of understanding of this critical issue by the current administration. ■

⇒ | ⇐

The Korean Crisis Demonstrates the Need for a Strong United States Navy

In response to North Korea's unprovoked and brutal artillery attack on a South Korean fishing village earlier this week, President Obama did what American presidents have done for over half a century: he dispatched a carrier strike group to the crisis zone. The *USS George Washington* and its escort ships will patrol the Yellow Sea to reassure our Korean allies and serve notice upon North Korea that it is within reach of American naval airpower. Such an option may not be available to Mr. Obama's successors, however, if the administration's deep cuts to the Navy's shipbuilding budget continue.

Watching the decline of the US Navy from its Cold War-dominating, 600-ship level to today's 286-ship fleet, China has sensed its opportunity to expand its reach in the Pacific, especially in the Yellow Sea, where the *George Washington* is headed. China has declared the South and East China Seas and Yellow Sea within its "core interests." To back up its claims to large swaths of the Pacific once protected by the US Navy, China has engaged in a massive ship and submarine building spree and intends to launch four aircraft carriers in the coming decade. On Friday, China's state-run Xinhua news agency reported that China had warned the

This article was originally published in the *Daily Caller*, November 30, 2010.

United States against "any military acts in [its] exclusive economic zone without permission." Since this zone includes most of the international waters in the Yellow Sea, China has essentially told Mr. Obama to recall the *USS George Washington* from its current mission. So far, Mr. Obama has not bowed to the edict.

China has put the United States on notice before that it does not appreciate interference in its self-proclaimed backyard. Most dramatically, in October 2006, a 160-foot Chinese Song-class diesel-electric attack submarine surfaced within torpedo and missile firing range of the *USS Kitty Hawk,* having stalked the American aircraft carrier and evaded its defensive screen. The incident was widely reported in the international press and reportedly caused major embarrassment to the Pentagon. The following year, the Chinese denied the *Kitty Hawk* entry to Hong Kong's Victoria Harbor, where the ship was seeking refuge from building seas and deteriorating weather.

Chinese harassment of the US Navy has not been confined to the *Kitty Hawk.* On March 4, 2009, a Chinese Bureau of Fisheries Patrol vessel used a spotlight to illuminate the *USNS Victorious* and crossed the American vessel's bow at a range of 1,400 yards at night without notice or warning. The next day, a Chinese Y-12 maritime surveillance aircraft conducted twelve fly-bys of the *Victorious* at low altitude.

In the same week, a Chinese frigate approached the *USNS Impeccable* and proceeded to cross its bow at a range of approximately one hundred yards. Two hours later, a Chinese Y-12 conducted eleven fly-bys over the *Impeccable* at low altitude. Two days after that, five Chinese ships surrounded and harassed the *Impeccable* in the South China Sea.

In an April 2009 incident that foreshadowed the recent ramming of a Japanese Coast Guard boat by a Chinese "fishing" trawler, two Chinese fishing vessels came dangerously close to a US military ship in the Yellow Sea off the coast of China, one of several similar incidents that have taken place, according to Navy officials.

Chinese conventional, nuclear attack, and ballistic missile submarines, new "carrier killer" missiles, and under-construction aircraft carriers are being deployed to limit the operating areas of American air and naval forces with an intent to weaken the bond between the United States and its regional friends and allies, such as South Korea. If America does not immediately reverse the decline of its naval fleet, in a future crisis, China might simply inform the American president that sending a carrier to South Korea or some other hot spot in the region is no longer an option. Unlike today, the United States may not have the capability to ignore such an order. That would be a sad day indeed for the United States and its allies. ■

≋ | ≋

Is This the End of the Royal Navy?

It is hard to tell at this point who is the biggest winner from this week's decimation of the United Kingdom's Ministry of Defense and slashing of the Royal Navy's budget. British Navy chiefs are confirming that after losing their only current carrier at the end of this year, *HMS Ark Royal*, the United Kingdom will not have a fully operational aircraft carrier until 2036. After the devastating cuts, the British Navy will be at its smallest size since the time of Henry VIII and will be roughly half the size of the current French Navy.

The Russians could not be more pleased. For decades, British carriers of the Invincible-class have been a sturdy cork keeping Russia's Northern Fleet bottled up in the Barents Sea. Without the air power and anti-submarine warfare capabilities of its light carrier force, Britain's coast-guard-sized collection of frigates and destroyers will be little match for Russia's powerful surface ships and nuclear subs, which will now have open access to the North Atlantic.

Argentina and its Chavez-supporting first couple must also be thrilled that the Falklands—or should we now just start calling them Las Islas Malvinas?—will no longer have the protection of a British fleet that could deploy airpower to the South Atlantic. That hearty band of British sheep farmers and, now, oil and gas prospectors—who have no interest

This article was originally published on *CBSNews.com*, October 22, 2010.

in becoming Argentine citizens—must be very nervous. Perhaps Prime Minister Cameron might just consider negotiating the surrender of the islands now to avoid the embarrassment of being defeated by Argentine forces with a Venezuelan expeditionary unit in support. He might even get a small oil royalty payment in return.

China always seems to be a winner these days and is again now. Instead of the United States being able to rely on a robust British presence in the Atlantic that would have allowed it to shift more warships and carriers to the Pacific, the United States must continue to split its dwindling naval resources between the two oceans. China's announcement last week that it is launching thirty new patrol boats in the aftermath of the Senkaku Island incident with Japan makes the British cuts even harder for the West to bear.

Of course, the French, Spanish, and Italian navies will also be happy that their forces all will have more capacity and outnumber the vaunted Royal Navy. This may allow the European Union to further integrate the United Kingdom into its super-state, as Britain will be forced to rely on other navies' carriers and amphibious ships to land Royal Marines on foreign shores or to rescue British citizens in crisis zones such as Britain has previously done—on its own—in places such as Lebanon and Sierra Leone.

While Britain turns inward and disarms, America and its remaining naval allies cannot afford to close their eyes on the increasingly dangerous world in which we live. In the coming years, China alone will launch four super carriers, two of them nuclear-powered. Russia is also using its mineral and oil wealth to reactivate its carrier program. Iran and other littoral states are deploying scores of small boats and, like the Chinese, are making extravagant claims regarding their territorial waters. The freedom of global navigation and the seas are at risk.

Last month, I predicted that the United Kingdom would try to sell one of its new carriers. That is apparently now the case. In an article for the *Australian Conservative*, I urged that Australia step forward to purchase the warship. The United States and Britain, for that matter, should do all that they can to assist Australia in reaching that conclusion. America needs a robust allied navy that it can depend on in any crisis. Australia will have to take over that role from the Royal Navy, at least in the South Pacific.

India, which is being encircled by a network of Chinese-built ports and possible future naval bases, and is confronted by Islamic extremists operating from neighboring Pakistan, has a history of operating British-built light carriers. The current flagship aircraft carrier of the Indian Navy, *INS Viraat*, is the former *HMS Hermes*, and has a complement of Harrier jets. India has demonstrated a commitment to freedom of the seas and understands that it will have to confront Chinese domination of the Indian Ocean and continued terrorism in the region. The Indian Navy would be an excellent home for the newly decommissioned *Ark Royal*. There, the ship and its aircraft could be put to great use defending sea lanes and defeating terrorists.

The United States must understand that its traditional allies in Europe are not going to increase their contribution to global security, especially in guaranteeing the freedom of the seas. Accordingly, it is time for the United States to end the Obama administration's decommissioning spree with the US Navy. Last month, America announced that eight additional warships would be taken out of service. The navy's shipbuilding budget is chronically underfunded. Both trends must be reversed now. America must recommit to its Navy.

The United Kingdom is facing the results of decades of welfare state overspending and its armed forces and global security are paying the price. It is not, however, too late for Prime Minister Cameron to change course and reverse the cuts to the Royal Navy. It would be incredibly sad to see that great institution, which has survived onslaughts by the Spanish Armada, the French Navy, and the German High Seas Fleet, be done in by Tory accountants. ■

SECTION 4

≡ | ≋

China
Red Storm Rising

SECTION 4

Ensuring China's Peaceful Rise

President Barack Obama's recent trip to Honolulu to attend the APEC summit is merely the latest step in what Secretary of State Hillary Clinton has dubbed a "pivot," or refocus, of American interests in Asia. But as the United States looks to follow through on the pledge so clearly outlined by Clinton in her *Foreign Policy* essay in September, attention is again inevitably turning to Asia's looming economic and military giant: China.

There has been much discussion and speculation in recent commentary over China's rapid maritime rise and strategy for dominating large swaths of the Pacific, including one I recently penned for the *Diplomat*. China's maritime rise is symbolized by the sea trials this summer of its first aircraft carrier, the ex-Ukrainian *Varyag*, the launch of which is part of a shipbuilding program not seen since Kaiser Wilhelm II ordered Imperial Germany's High Seas Fleet at the turn of the last century.

China's naval buildup will soon give Beijing the means to use military force to back up its expansive territorial claims to essentially the entire Yellow Sea, East China Sea, and South China Sea. In response, Southeast Asian nations, Japan, India, and Australia have all embarked on significant defense force modernization programs of their own, increasing their

---

This article was originally published in the *Diplomat*, November 19, 2011.

budgets for major air and naval platforms. Submarines are in particular demand.

Despite using the term "peaceful rise" for almost a decade to describe its global diplomatic, economic, and military growth, China hasn't hesitated to support its territorial claims in the Pacific with what senior American officials have repeatedly labeled as "aggressive" naval action by the People's Liberation Army (PLA) Navy, Air Force, and auxiliary forces. While individual incidents at sea have been reported in regional, maritime, military or, on occasion, the mainstream press, the full extent of China's efforts to exert control over nearby international waters hasn't been widely covered in the West. Governments, on the other hand, are increasingly concerned about China's naval behavior in the region. Indeed, Japan accused Beijing, for the first time, of "assertiveness" in an official government white paper issued in July. Japan's characterization of Chinese action in an official government document is certainly blunt in "diplospeak."

As China asserts its claims in the Pacific, it has made no secret of its opposition to US freedom-of-navigation operations in nearby international waters, and it hasn't confined its unhappiness to mere diplomatic protests. Instead, Chinese forces have confronted the world's leading navy at sea in some well-publicized incidents.

Such challenges aren't wholly new. The first major incident between US and PLA forces occurred just several years after the fall of the Soviet Union. In July and August 1995 and March 1996, in response to certain measures in Taiwan interpreted by China as moves toward Taiwanese independence, China conducted "missile tests and other military exercises" near the Taiwan Strait. In March 1996, the United States responded by sending two carrier strike groups toward the region. China seemingly backed away from confrontation, but many analysts have suggested this was a turning point in PLA thinking.

Tensions would again escalate shortly after the inauguration of President George W. Bush in 2001. The Chinese interception of an American EP-3 surveillance aircraft flying in international airspace over the East China Sea forced the damaged plane to land at a Chinese military base, triggering a diplomatic incident.

In October 2006, the *USS Kitty Hawk* was stalked by a 160-foot Chinese Song-class diesel-electric attack submarine, which culminated in the surfacing of the Chinese sub within torpedo firing range of the US carrier. More recently, in late June of this year, Chinese Sukhoi-27 fighters shadowed an American reconnaissance plane, causing Taiwan to scramble two F-16 fighters to intercept the Chinese jets near the central line across the 113-mile-wide strait, the first such incursion by China in twelve years.

But the United States isn't the only country to have been on the receiving end of Chinese assertiveness. In March, two Chinese gunboats tried to drive away a Philippines Department of Energy research vessel from the Reed Bank in the vicinity of the Kalayaan Island group, controlled by the Philippines, which is part of the Spratly Islands. The incident prompted the Philippine government to file a diplomatic protest, which China summarily dismissed. In May, Chinese ships allegedly cut cables on a Hanoi-chartered survey vessel working for foreign oil and gas exploration firms in the South China Sea.

One of the most famous "incidents" relates to reports that circulated from July of this year, when the Indian amphibious ship *Airavat* was on a show-the-flag mission before being challenged as it sailed from Vietnam's Nha Trang port near Cam Ranh Bay. A purported Chinese naval officer reportedly radioed the ship that it was entering Chinese waters as it approached Haiphong. While it's likely that the PLA Navy made no such call, the incident has "calcified into fact among Indian commentators" and underscores the danger that incidents at sea can escalate.

As the United States and Asian nations now consider the implications of China's massive naval buildup and expansive territorial claims in the Pacific, they must do so in light of China's proven willingness to use its armed forces as a means to enforce such claims. The list of incidents at sea involving the PLA Navy, Air Force, and auxiliary forces is especially remarkable in that the confrontations have taken place during a period in which the US Navy has been dominant in the region.

As the PLA Navy continues its impressive growth, and as the US Navy shrinks as a result of significant cuts in American defense spending, it's quite possible that Chinese-initiated confrontations will increase if the PLA Navy determines that the balance of forces in the region has tilted in China's favor. Indeed, China's party-controlled press seems to foreshadow such a situation. Discussing the refusal of Asian nations to accede to China's South China Sea "core interest" claims, China's Communist Party newspaper warned last month that if neighboring nations "don't change their ways with China, they will need to mentally prepare for the sound of cannons. We need to be ready for that, as it may be the only way for the disputes in the sea to be resolved." This course is fraught with peril for not only the United States and Asian nations, but for an assertive China as well.

In responding to China's assertiveness, the United States and Asian nations should recognize that maintaining a balance of forces, in which the risk of escalation is too great for China to engage in such conduct, is the best way to deter potentially violent incidents at sea. In an era of a smaller US Navy, achieving this balance can be accomplished, for example, by deploying a greater percentage of American naval resources to the Pacific. This approach is already underway, but should be complemented by encouraging our regional allies to build and/or purchase the air and naval platforms necessary to defend themselves. These allies could also increase their training tempo and the number of joint exercises with the United States military to ensure smooth joint operations in the event of a future conflict.

Yet despite the obvious advantage of assisting the efforts of its friends to enhance their defensive capabilities, the United States has refused to sell Japan and Australia, two of its closest allies, the F-22 Raptor, a fifth-generation fighter jet. The United States also bowed to Chinese pressure and refused to sell Taiwan the F-16C/D variant Fighting Falcon, which is a defensive fourth-generation fighter jet. The refusal to arm our allies sends the wrong message to China and our allies. Of course, it also undermines the American military-industrial base, which is already under siege from large cuts in the US defense budget.

On the diplomatic front, the United States must make clear that it will scrupulously honor its defense treaty commitments to Pacific partners such as Australia, Japan, and the Philippines. The United States should also continue to side with Association of Southeast Asian Nations (ASEAN), which seeks to protect its member nations' maritime rights under international law and their rights to freely navigate international waters. ASEAN's effort to implement the 2002 Declaration of Conduct of Parties in the South China Sea is also worthy of American support. The July 2011 Bali guidelines are a small step forward on this front, but more must be done. Backed by American diplomacy, ASEAN's hand in its negotiations with China on the Declaration of Conduct will be strengthened.

The best ally of peace in the Pacific is a strong United States that is committed to working with its allies to ensure that China's maritime rise really is a peaceful one. ∎

SECTION 4

≡ | ≡

China's Two-Pronged Maritime Rise

For the past decade, while the West has been consumed battling Islamic extremists in the Middle East and Central Asia, China has been engaged in a rapid and impressive effort to establish itself as the supreme maritime power in the eastern Pacific and Indian Oceans.

For years, China focused its military spending on the People's Liberation Army, while its air force and navy served as little more than adjuncts to the army. But with the launch of its first aircraft carrier next month, the rest of the world—and especially the United States' Asian allies—is taking note of how dramatically things have changed. China has significant maritime ambitions, and they are backed up by a naval buildup unseen since Kaiser Wilhelm II decided to challenge British naval power with the building of the High Seas Fleet at the turn of the last century.

China's buildup is driven by a two-pronged strategy. First, China seeks to deny access by the United States and other naval powers to the Yellow, East China, and South China Seas, thereby (1) establishing its own equivalent to the way the United States saw the Caribbean in the twentieth century, from which its blue-water navy can operate globally; (2) dominating the natural resources and disputed island chains such as the Spratly and Senkaku Island chains in those seas; and (3) giving it

---

This article was originally published in the *Diplomat*, July 24, 2011.

the capacity to reunify Taiwan with the mainland by force and without US interference, if necessary. China's assertiveness in confronting and harassing Asian and American civilian and naval ships in the region over the past decade shows a sustained level of determination on this front.

Second, China seeks international prestige and a power projection capacity in the Pacific and Indian Ocean sea lanes by deploying multiple aircraft carriers and fifth-generation stealth fighter-bombers. The booming Chinese economy has become ever more dependent on imported minerals and oil from Africa and the Middle East, and the ability to protect its Indian Ocean and Strait of Malacca sea lanes is a responsibility that China is no longer willing to delegate to other powers.

The officially reported Chinese military budget for 2011 is $91.5 billion, a massive increase from its $14.6 billion budget in 2000. China acknowledges that one-third of its spending is now devoted to its navy, yet even this big leap is almost certainly understated. China is notoriously non-transparent with its military expenditures, and most analysts believe that it spends significantly more on its armed forces than the publicly reported number. Further, Chinese military labor costs for its soldiers, sailors, and airmen is a fraction of what Western governments spend, where salaries, benefits and pensions are usually the largest share of defense budgets. This allows China to devote more of its budget to building weapons systems than its competitors. Unlike Western governments, which are slashing defense spending, China will continue to increase spending in coming years.

A key goal of China's maritime buildup is access denial. While multifaceted, China is building its access denial strategy around two backbone platforms: the DF-21D (Dong Feng) anti-ship ballistic missile (ASBM), described as a "carrier killer," and an ever-expanding and modern attack submarine fleet. US Navy Pacific Commander Admiral Robert F. Willard has characterized the DF-21D as already having reached the Initial Operational Capability stage of development, meaning that it is operable, but not yet necessarily deployable. Taiwan sources report that China has already deployed at least twenty ASBMs. Whether deployed now or in the near future, the US Navy believes China already has the space-based intelligence, surveillance and reconnaissance, command and control structure, and ground processing capabilities necessary to support DF-21D employment. China also employs an array of non-space-based sensors and surveillance assets capable of providing the targeting information necessary to employ the DF-21D. With a recently reported range of 2,600 kilometers, these missiles will give naval planners real concern when operating anywhere near the Chinese mainland.

The Chinese submarine program has been especially vigorous. For most of the Cold War, China operated outdated Soviet-era coastal submarines. In the 1990s, China purchased Russian Kilo-class diesel-electric attack submarines, and has been launching two indigenously built Song-class diesel-electric attack submarines per year for the past decade. It has also developed and launched the high-tech Yuan-class diesel-electric attack boat, which may have the silent air-independent propulsion system. Analysts believe that China will in the coming years also launch the Shang-class nuclear-powered attack submarine, further strengthening its already robust submarine fleet. It has surely not escaped China's notice that US anti-submarine warfare capability has atrophied significantly since the end of the Cold War.

But China's maritime capabilities are set to extend beyond access denial, into power projection. The systems that have gained the most international attention are China's planned aircraft carriers and its new fifth-generation fighter bomber. Any time now, the PLA Navy will commence sea trials for its first carrier, the ex-Ukrainian *Varyag*, which has been renamed *Shi Lang*. The former Soviet ship is larger than European carriers, but one-third smaller than US Nimitz-class carriers. Moreover, China has publicly confirmed it has a second, larger, conventionally powered carrier under domestic construction that will likely be launched in 2015. China has planned or is constructing a third conventionally powered carrier and two nuclear-powered carriers are on the drawing board, with a planned completion date of 2020.

Equally important as the warships are the aircraft China plans to deploy on its flat tops. The main fighter-bomber in the PLA Navy carrier air wing will be the J-15 Flying Shark, which under current configuration is comparable in size and capability to the US Navy's retired F-14 Tomcat. The jet will have limited range, given its weight taking off from the ski-deck-configured *Shi Lang*; however, it's believed that advances in Chinese aeronautics and avionics, as well as a catapult launch system on forthcoming carriers, could put the J-15 in the same performance class as the American F-18 Super Hornet in the future. China may also have developed a carrier-based airborne warning and control systems (AWACS) aircraft, which would be a major development. An Internet-sourced photograph that appeared in mid-May, meanwhile, shows a corner of a model of what is clearly a small AWACS aircraft inspired by the E-2 Hawkeye and the unrealized Soviet Yak-44 designs.

To put China's carrier program in perspective, with the retirement of the *USS Enterprise* this summer, the United States will have only ten carriers to meet worldwide commitments; China will likely have five carriers devoted to the Asia-Pacific region alone. China's buildup is being noted even in the popular Western media, which has given significant coverage to China's prototype fifth-generation twin-engine stealth fighter-bomber, the J-20 Black Silk. The jet is larger than the USAF F-22 Raptor and could prove to be comparable in capability (although some US observers claim it is more similar to the slightly less sophisticated US and allied F-35 Joint Strike Fighter, which will be the frontline US carrier fighter).

The J-20 prototype took off on its maiden test flight in January from an airfield in the southwestern city of Chengdu, flying for about fifteen minutes on the same day then-US Defense Secretary Robert Gates was in Beijing meeting with Chinese President Hu Jintao, sending a strong political message and earning the jet a spot on evening news programs worldwide.

China is believed to have received a major assist in developing the J-20 by obtaining materials from a downed US F-117 Night Hawk from Serbia, as well as from the believed cyber theft of JSF plans from US defense contractors. (With this in mind, American planners should also assume that Chinese engineers have had access to the rotor tail of the stealth helicopter that was ditched in the Osama bin Laden raid in Pakistan).

These rapid and high-level technical achievements have apparently surprised many Western observers, and the consensus is that the West has consistently underestimated the strength of China's military-industrial capability and its determination to expand and modernize its armed forces, especially the PLA Navy. But it should now be more than clear that the world is facing a significant challenge to a maritime system that has been dominated for the past two hundred years by Anglo-American navies. How the United States responds to China's challenge will define the balance of power in the Asia-Pacific region for the rest of the century. ■

China's Africa Play

Twenty years ago, China's main concern in Africa was upending the diplomatic relations enjoyed by Taiwan with numerous sub-Saharan nations. Now China's unprecedented drive to take the preeminent role on the African continent is being fueled by its vast energy, mineral, and foodstuff requirements.

I just returned from a visit to South Africa. Earlier in the year I traveled to Rwanda and Kenya. One trend that is impossible to ignore in sub-Saharan Africa is the growing role China is taking in the continent's affairs. Beijing is on the move in Africa—using aid, diplomacy, weapons sales, and Chinese expats in a bid to become the preeminent power in the region.

The anecdotal evidence is everywhere. In Kigali, the big modern Chinese embassy bristles with communication antennae and dishes. Rwanda, with its paucity of natural resources, seems a surprising place for such an installation until you factor in the country's role as the gateway to the Eastern Congo and its untold mineral wealth. It has been widely reported that China recently purchased half the farmland under cultivation in the Congo.

Roads in Nairobi, notorious for their clogged traffic circles, are being widened and repaved with large billboards telling Kenyans that the work

This article was originally published on *CBSNews.com*, January 19, 2010.

is a gift from the people of China. The fact that the roads will ease congestion for Kenyan motorists is an afterthought to the benefactor, which requires modern infrastructure to move African commodities to ports for shipment to China.

Rural South African towns that have been losing population for two decades are seeing an influx of Chinese restaurateurs and merchants. A parliamentary leader in one South African province told me he believes that many of the small businessmen who have fanned out across his remote farming and mining constituency have ties to Chinese intelligence. In neighboring Namibia, China established its first overseas military base to track its satellite and manned space flights.

The *Wall Street Journal* reported this week that Chinese companies are considering the purchase of interests in Nigerian oil companies, including the stakes currently held by major American companies.

China's rapid inroads into Africa are made possible by a combination of Chinese money and a willingness by Beijing to deal with some of the world's most unsavory leaders and human rights abusers, such as Robert Mugabe in Zimbabwe and Omar Hassan Ahmad al-Bashir in the Sudan. The inattention of the West to this important development has made China's strategic initiative that much easier.

The prospect of an Africa dominated by China means that progress in human rights and democracy in the region will stall—and could be reversed. While propping up dictators may make doing business there easier, it will certainly ensure that corruption will continue to flourish and Africans will continue to be oppressed. Chinese money and weapons in the hands of those who have no problem using them to steal, stifle dissent, and subjugate minority tribes is a bad thing.

The United States and the West also require fair access to the vital energy supplies and strategic minerals in Africa. American policymakers have already identified West African oil reserves as a resource that can lessen our dependence on volatile Middle Eastern and Venezuelan markets. Undue Chinese political and economic influence on the continent could deny America access to these critical sources of supply in the future.

America is in a unique position to promote free men and free markets in Africa. The United States can compete with China diplomatically and commercially in the region. Unlike European countries, the United States does not carry baggage from a colonial past. Sub-Saharan Africa is a place where America remains truly popular. President Bush's HIV/AIDS initiative was very well received. The Millennium Development Corporation is better known there than here. The United States is led by a president of African descent who is widely admired on the continent, and American pop culture rules in Africa.

To stem the Chinese tide and to give Africans the opportunity to have a better future, the United States must strongly advocate for human rights, democracy, and freedom on the continent. We cannot be reticent to criticize African strongmen in forums such as the UN. The people of Africa are not looking for our apologies; they are looking for us to bolster them as they struggle against tyranny and corruption.

We should support those countries such as Botswana, Rwanda, and South Africa that are committed democracies—and nurture those, such as Liberia, that are making progress in the right direction with increased trade, investment, and tourism. The budget of the Millennium Development Corporation can be increased and focused on Africa. America should remain at the forefront of funding HIV/AIDS, polio vaccination, and anti-malaria programs on the continent. All of the foregoing programs have broad bipartisan support.

Further, the Africom HQ needs to move from Frankfurt to Africa. The HQ would immediately provide the host country with an economic boost. It would also allow us to work closely on the ground with the AU on peacekeeping logistics and training. Having our HQ in the region will encourage friends and cause the foes of freedom to be nervous. It will also demonstrate our ability to project power in a way the Chinese still cannot.

An African renaissance requires democracy, transparency, and respect for human rights. A free and transparent Africa will be a friendly place for the United States and a partner in trade and culture long into the future. An Africa dominated by China is unlikely to be such a partner. The time for America to fully engage in Africa is now. ■

⇒ | ⇐

The United States and China Vie for Influence in the Horn of Africa

While often under the mainstream media radar, East Africa is a national security and foreign policy hot spot for the United States.

African Union forces are fighting the militant Islamist insurgency Al-Shabaab in Mogadishu, Somalia, where the US- and UN-backed Transitional Federal Government is attempting to establish itself. Al-Shabaab has responded with suicide bombings in Uganda and has threatened other countries in the region. Combined Task Force 151, led by the EU, patrols the Indian Ocean attempting to stem Somali piracy, some of which is sponsored by Islamic terrorist groups. Yet the pirates brazenly continue to capture ships, including American vessels, as far away as the Seychelles and Mozambique. Terrorism experts report that all of East Africa is at high risk of al-Qaeda terrorist activity, with Kenya and Uganda being the leading targets.

After a week of voting in the Sudan, African Christians in the South are expected to have overwhelmingly cast their ballots for freedom from the Arab-dominated North that currently governs the country. Despite recent hopeful signals from Sudanese President Omar al-Bashir, few believe that Khartoum will allow the oil-rich South to leave Sudan without bloodshed.

This article was originally published in the *Daily Caller*, February 4, 2011.

Sudan's extensive oil reserves, new oil finds in Somalia and Uganda, and the region's rich mineral deposits also make East Africa a key strategic region for the global economy. As a commodities treasure chest, the region is of interest to China.

America's key ally with respect to all of these issues is Kenya. It is from Nairobi that the UN supports the Transitional Federal Government in Somalia. Somali pirates captured on the high seas are turned over to Kenyan courts for trial. Kenya has been an important supporter of the South Sudanese government and has reportedly trained its defense forces. The Kenyan National Security Intelligence Service (NSIS), which was formed in the aftermath of the 1998 bombing of the US Embassy in Nairobi, has assisted American law enforcement agencies in arresting a number of terrorists in the country. As a member of the British Commonwealth and a parliamentary democracy, Kenya has traditionally been an ally of the West and wary of Russian or Chinese initiatives in Africa.

Consequently, it was not helpful last month when Kenyan daily newspapers splashed classified US State Department cables disclosed by WikiLeaks on their front pages. Papers touting headlines such as "The Secret Files" and "Revealed: [US] Envoy's Road Map for 'Regime Change'" were hawked by newsboys and snapped up by Kenyans on busy Nairobi traffic circles. One cable from Embassy Nairobi reportedly stated that "most of the political and economic elite compose the vested interests that benefit from and support impunity and the lack of accountability with respect to governance, state resources, and the rule of law. This includes President Kibaki and Prime Minister Odinga..."

According to the *Daily Nation*, just prior to the release of the cables by WikiLeaks, US Assistant Secretary of State for Africa Johnnie Carson called the Kenyan prime minister to warn him about the leaked cables and to apologize for some of the comments contained therein. Putting aside the merits of the embassy's reporting from Kenya, the effect of the leaked cables could seriously damage American relations with its important partner in East Africa at a critical time. Fortunately for the United States, for now, the Kenyan government has publicly brushed the matter aside. Assistant Secretary Carson's telephone diplomacy may have averted a freeze in relations.

A second major story from the leaked cables describing China's adventures in Kenya also received significant press coverage. Although denied by the Kenyan government, the cables alleged that China was paying Kenyan security service agents for influence and had provided the Kenyan intelligence agency with computers and telecommunications monitoring equipment, which were being serviced by Chinese technicians working on site.

The *Daily Nation* also reported that the Kenyan Wildlife Service claims 90 percent of the ivory poachers it detains are Chinese and that poaching increases whenever a Chinese labor camp is established in Kenya. By exposing the dark side of China's incursion into Kenya, the leaks confirmed to ordinary Kenyans that China's interest in the region is not entirely benevolent.

China's longtime support of Sudan's war crimes-indicted leader Omar al-Bashir in exchange for easy access to Sudanese oil, and close association with other strongmen in Africa, demonstrates a lack of regard for human rights and democracy on the continent. Even its motives for involvement in anti-piracy naval efforts off Somalia have been called into question by Western naval officers, who report that China seems more interested in learning Western naval tactics than fighting pirates.

At a time when so many key Western interests are affected by events in East Africa, it is critically important for the United States to remain fully engaged in the region and to support our African allies. It is clear that China has recognized the importance of the region and is looking to supplant the United States as superpower-in-residence. Should this occur, both America and Africa will be worse off. ■

China's Next Move
A Naval Base in the South Atlantic?

I recently returned from Walvis Bay, Namibia, the country's sole deep-water port and former South Atlantic home to the Royal and South African Navies. Also in port were two of the three ships of the Royal Navy's Atlantic Patrol Tasking South. A Daring-class Type 45 air warfare destroyer and a Royal Fleet Auxiliary small fleet tanker were both pier side. (The task force's third ship, *HMS Clyde*, was presumably on station patrolling the Falklands.) While Walvis Bay enjoys a 138-year history with the Royal Navy, it could soon be home to a powerful Chinese People's Liberation Army (PLA) Navy surface squadron.

In January 2015, the *Namibian* reported the existence of a "confidential letter from Namibia's ambassador to China, Ringo Abed, to Namibia's foreign minister stat[ing] that 'a [Chinese] delegation will visit Namibia ... for discussions ... on the way forward regarding plans for the proposed naval base in Walvis Bay.'" According to the letter, a Chinese delegation, including technical staff and naval architects, would meet with Namibian officials sometime after March 21, 2015 to discuss a field feasibility study for the base. Beijing has told Namibian diplomats that a "Chinese naval presence will deter any would-be illegal trawlers and smugglers." China's Indian Ocean-based "string of pearls" naval base strategy to protect the country's twenty-first-century vision of a "maritime silk road" looks like it

This article was originally published on *RealClearDefense.com*, March 25, 2015.

may now extend all the way to the South Atlantic. If such a development came to fruition, it would have major strategic implications for the West.

During my visit to Walvis Bay, China's plan to build a naval base was the talk of the town. Several Namibians pointed out that China already has a major satellite tracking installation in the country. China is developing key uranium mines. Chinese immigrants are opening shops in every corner of the land. A Namibian told me he would not be surprised if Namibia soon elects its first Chinese member of parliament. One local, who works at the harbor, said he has heard the PLA Navy will deploy four to six warships to the prospective base. Once that happens, he said, Namibia becomes, in essence, a Chinese colony. That estimate is consistent with a reported PLA Navy call on Walvis Bay last year, which said: "PLAN's 16th escort task force consisting of the Taihu, a Type 903 replenishment ship, Yancheng, a Type 054A guided-missile frigate and Luoyang, a Type 053H3 frigate, anchored in Walvis Bay during a mission to the Gulf of Aden."

This history of Walvis Bay is dictated by its strategic importance as a naval station. Britain occupied Walvis Bay in 1838 to keep the deepwater harbor out of the Kaiser's hands. It allowed the territory to be annexed by the Cape Colony in the same year. Briefly overrun by the Germans in 1915, South Africa recaptured Walvis Bay during the World War I Southwest Africa campaign. The naval base at Walvis Bay remained in the Royal Navy's hands until South Africa became a republic in 1960. Even after Namibia gained its independence in 1990, Walvis Bay stayed South African sovereign territory. South Africa only ceded Walvis Bay to Namibia as an act of African solidarity after Nelson Mandela was elected president in 1994.

The South Atlantic, while below the radar of most policymakers today, has played an outsize role in modern naval history. Therein lies the importance of Walvis Bay. At the outset of World War I, on December 8, 1914, the Royal Navy defeated the Imperial German Navy's then-famous Pacific Cruiser Squadron, under the command of Admiral Graf Maximilian von Spee, in the Battle of the Falkland Islands. The British victory prevented Spee from wreaking havoc on allied merchant shipping in the Atlantic as he had done in the Pacific.

The Battle of the River Plate in the South Atlantic on December 13, 1939, was the first major naval engagement of World War II. Four Royal

Navy cruisers engaged the German pocket battleship, *Graf Spee*, after it had sunk several allied merchant ships near St. Helena Island in the South Atlantic. The German warship was scuttled by its crew in the River Plate after it was cornered by the Royal Navy. Later in the war, during the Battle of the Atlantic, allied long-range naval patrol flying boats and land-based aircraft operated from Ascension and St. Helena Islands, performing anti-surface commerce raider and anti-submarine warfare missions.

In 1982, British Prime Minister Margaret Thatcher assembled the most powerful naval battle group since World War II and dispatched it to the South Atlantic to retake the Falklands from Argentina, which had illegally invaded and occupied the islands. After the nuclear hunter submarine *HMS Conqueror* sank the Argentine battle cruiser *General Belgrano* on May 2, 1982, Argentina ceased to be anything close to a blue-water naval force of any consequence in the region.

During one of the last hot conflicts of the Cold War, the Angolan civil war, Fidel Castro was exceedingly anxious that the South African Navy, based at Walvis Bay, would attack and sink his troop and armament conveys bound for Angola's capital, Luanda. South Africa retired its last blue-water frigate, *President Pretorius*, in July 1985 due to budgetary issues. Nevertheless, Castro was concerned by South Africa's small fleet of Daphne-class diesel-electric submarines that sometimes deployed from Walvis Bay.

Since the mid-1980s, when the South Atlantic's regional powers—Argentina and South Africa—basically stopped policing the ocean's blue waters, the job has fallen primarily to Britain. The United Kingdom has the most significant Western interests in the region. According to the Royal Navy, Atlantic Patrol Tasking South "provide[s] ongoing protection and reassurance to British interests [and "allied nations"] in the South Atlantic, maintaining the continuous Royal Naval presence in the Atlantic." For decades, the United Kingdom has protected the vital South Atlantic sea lanes as well as its territories of Ascension, St. Helena, and the oil-rich Falklands and related islands on a very efficient basis with just one Type 45 destroyer (albeit likely the most sophisticated destroyer in the world) or a Type 23 frigate. The lone warship is usually accompanied by a replenishment ship when on extended deployment in the South Atlantic. Given the significant cuts to the Royal Navy since Prime Minister Cameron took office amid the global financial crisis, coupled with Britain's other commitments, one warship is probably the most the Royal Navy can deploy to the South Atlantic. The US Navy, its own fleet size declining for years and preoccupied with the Middle East and Pacific, has been pleased to see its closest naval ally provide presence in the region.

In this context, China's desire to extend its growing surface warfare fleet to a Walvis Bay base is smart geopolitical and naval strategy—amplified by the fact that Beijing has already showed at least some interest in the Atlantic going back to late 2012. Namibia is a friendly government that will be increasingly susceptible to Chinese influence as the PLA's bases there grow—as do the Chinese immigrant population and China's commercial mining investments.

Across the South Atlantic, Argentina is hostile to Britain due to the Falklands territorial dispute. Buenos Aires is also antagonistic to America and various European nations as a result of a massive bond crisis. Accordingly, Chinese warships should have ample opportunities for port visits and to conduct joint exercises across the ocean from its hoped-for base at Walvis Bay. Recent press reports also claim that China is negotiating to sell jet fighters to Argentina. If the deal is completed, those fighters would pose a direct threat to Britain's air superiority over the Falklands. Such a deal would also almost certainly result in a contingent of PLA Air Force personnel taking up residence in Argentina for training and maintenance purposes.

The other regional player, South Africa, has a robust small fleet but its combat readiness and effectiveness have been questioned in recent years. Further, South Africa's post-apartheid government has maintained strong and friendly ties with Beijing over the past two decades. Thus, South Africa can no longer be counted on as a ready Western ally in the event of a crisis involving China. And, access to its naval bases at Simonstown, Port Elizabeth, and Durban cannot be taken for granted by NATO navies in such an event.

From a base at Walvis Bay, PLA Navy warships would have short distances to sail for friendly, if not allied, ports. It would have the ability to patrol the critical Cape of Good Hope around Africa and Cape Horn around South America. The approaches to the key North Atlantic sea lanes linking the Americas, Africa, and Europe would be nearby. Both Germany and the Soviet Union would have coveted such a naval base in the twentieth century. China is on the threshold of obtaining such an advantage in the twenty-first century.

Should the United States or United Kingdom fail to persuade Namibia to not allow China to build a naval base at Walvis Bay—or worse yet, not even engage on the issue—the West is not without resources should it later decide to counter China's South Atlantic gambit. The value of the airfields at the British Overseas Territories in the event of a South Atlantic crisis cannot be overestimated. The Royal Air Force's Mount Pleasant airbase in the Falklands is a massive hardened and fortified complex, nicknamed the "Death Star" by locals. The base could accommodate far more planes than the four Eurofighter Typhoons and Voyager tanker/transport now deployed there. Mount Pleasant is a strategic asset in the South Atlantic.

The RAF also manages Wideawake airfield on Ascension Island, which it describes as "an invaluable link and airhead for the South Atlantic, especially the Falkland Islands and St. Helena." The US Air Force already uses Wideawake airfield on a regular basis for a variety of contingencies and is very familiar with Ascension Island.

A new airport on St. Helena, Britain's second oldest colony, has been under construction since early 2012. It is scheduled to open next year at a cost to the United Kingdom of £201.5 million. The airport is slated for civilian use and will be managed by a South African concern, but the modern facility will be able to handle the entire range of NATO military aircraft. St. Helena's proximity to Walvis Bay is advantageous for ISR purposes.

Bermuda is the fourth important British possession in the region. The island provided key naval and air facilities in both world wars. It has a modern airport and harbor and can be readily supplied from the continental United States.

Mount Pleasant, Ascension, St. Helena, and Bermuda would provide excellent coverage over the South Atlantic for long-range naval patrol aircraft and bombers. Since its decision to scrap its Nimrod program, the United Kingdom no longer has a long-range naval aviation patrol capability. And, with the retirement of its Canberra and Vulcan bombers, the RAF no longer has a long-range bomber platform. Accordingly, it would fall to the United States to fly P-8 Poseidons from Britain's island airfields in order to effectively patrol the South Atlantic. The US Navy could also task surface combatants and submarines to augment the Royal Navy's patrol in the South Atlantic. In such a case, the islands would be available to surface combatants for resupply and limited maintenance requirements.

Of course, such deployments would heavily tax the shrinking US fleet and naval aviation assets and likely slow America's pivot to the Pacific. Thus, at relatively little cost to itself, a Chinese pivot to the South Atlantic via another "pearl" base at Walvis Bay could make America's already slow Pacific pivot all the more difficult.

Further, a robust PLA Navy presence in the South Atlantic could cause the United Kingdom to seek an accommodation with China in order to protect its last important overseas territories. China, which will be dependent on fossil fuels for decades to come, would certainly be interested in stakes in the rich offshore oil and gas fields surrounding the Falklands. It is not inconceivable that Whitehall could see involving China in such projects, backed up by the PLA Navy's South Atlantic presence, as a way of deterring Argentine aggression in the Falklands. As the United Kingdom continues to cut its defense budget as part of an overall effort to reduce the size of government, this might be seen as a low-cost way of maintaining British interests in the region. It is likely mere coincidence, but the timing of Britain's announcement that it will defy Washington and join China's Asia Infrastructure Investment Bank just as a PLA Navy delegation prepares for a visit to Namibia will not be lost on Beijing.

China is putting the South Atlantic into play with an audacious and clever geopolitical move to Walvis Bay. Consequently, after years off stage, the ocean that is famous for high-profile naval engagements may be making a comeback. ∎

SECTION 4

⇛ | ⇚

Africa Scenes

I wrote the below e-mail to my wife and kids on my BlackBerry in the back of a Land Cruiser in the Great Lakes region of Africa during a 2009 visit. I shared it with several colleagues who suggested that I post it on my web page. Africa remains one of the last places of true adventure in the world. For all of its challenges, the continent is an amazing place.

> Burnt wood smell in the air; VW bus taxis packed tighter than a fra-
> ternity prank; beat-up motor bikes weave through traffic with paying
> passengers on back; boys in orange vests sell newspapers and dodge
> traffic in the middle of intersections; Land Rovers and Cruisers, a few
> with snorkels announcing that they go up-country; women walk next
> to rural red dirt roads with plastic jugs and bags of flour on their heads
> and no destination in sight; banana and coffee plantations; bottled water
> in your briefcase; morning begins with Currie Cup rugby and English
> county cricket on in-room TV; passion fruit at the breakfast buffet in
> the five-star hotel for foreigners and big shots; diplomats, do-gooders,
> and foreign military officers mingle in the lobby; Chinese business-
> men huddle over coffee with their local agents in the not-yet-open bar;
> outside, UN and NGO compounds buzz behind red brick walls topped

This article was originally published on *robertcobrien.com*, July 15, 2009.

by poorly installed concertina wire; local HQ for British American Tobacco down the block; bored soldiers, AKs slung over shoulders, lounge against guard huts in front of Ministry buildings—don't photograph!; a sleek Engen petrol station sits next to a corrugated tin flat-roofed, mud-walled store selling Coca-Cola in eight-ounce tin cans, local beer, and individual cigarettes; young men squat against a wall painted with latest Vodaphone ad; clear, starry sky; warm tropical night; thatched-roof restaurant with an endless wood bar serves tasty grilled fish, curry, and goat to the stylish local urban elite, expats, and tourists in full khaki bush regalia and ... tennis shoes; Nigerian soccer league on TV overhead; endless talk of politics, corrupt leaders in neighboring states, and always a reason to blame France, Britain, or Belgium for some root-cause colonial evil; heartbreaking sadness caused by war, drought, and mosquitoes and yet the most cheerful smiles, warmth and kindness from the people ... This is Africa. You have to love it. ■

SECTION 5

⇒ | ⇐

Losing the War on Terror

≋ | ≋

Don't Give Guantánamo to Castro

L ast month, I traveled to the US naval base at Guantánamo Bay (GTMO) to see the Joint Task Force's (JTF) detention facilities and to receive a briefing on detainee issues from the JTF commander. I am the second person in my family to have visited GTMO. My father deployed to the base as a young Marine Corps officer during the Cuban Missile Crisis.

GTMO is the oldest American base overseas and the only US base in a Communist country. It is strategically located on the southeast corner of Cuba near the entrance of the Windward Passage, the strait that separates Cuba from Hispaniola. GTMO is a mere four hundred miles south of Miami. Through two world wars and the Cold War, GTMO has been a key to American control of sea lanes in the Caribbean that lead to the Panama Canal. In addition to its current role in the war on terror, the base allowed the United States to deal effectively with both the Cuban and Haitian refugee crises in the 1990s. GTMO continues to provide key support to the US Coast Guard's drug interdiction efforts in the region as it regularly hosts and supplies Coast Guard cutters and air crews during their patrols.

Cuba and the United States entered into the original base lease in 1903; it was reaffirmed in the Treaty of Relations ratified by Cuba and

---

This article was originally published on *Newsmax.com*, November 11, 2009.

the United States in 1934. The United States pays Cuba $4,085 per year to lease the property and keeps the bay's waterway dredged to allow commercial shipping to reach the Cuban commercial ports in the Ensenada de Joa. The lease can only be terminated with the agreement of both the United States and Cuba.

On his first day of office, January 22, 2009, President Barack Obama signed an executive order mandating the closure—within one year—of detention facilities for enemy combatants being held at GTMO. The order was issued notwithstanding the facts that most of the remaining detainees at GTMO are unrepentant terrorists and the conditions of their confinement are excellent, in full compliance with America's international treaty obligations, which are monitored by the International Committee of the Red Cross.

With the deadline for closing GTMO less than four months away, Congress has not yet approved funding for the move and a new site for these dangerous detainees has not yet been selected. Nevertheless, it is widely believed that at least a substantial number of the detainees will be moved to the United States by the president's deadline. Although time is short to plan and execute such a complicated logistics operation, our military will salute smartly and figure out a way to make it happen.

Having won the battle to close the detention facilities and to transfer the detainees to the United States, the left has now moved to its end game with respect to GTMO. It is demanding that our naval base be handed over to the Castro brothers' regime. On January 28, the Castros' mouthpiece, Cuban Foreign Minister Pérez Roque, told the *Agence France-Presse* that Cuba "expects that Obama's decision to close down the Guantanamo prison camp 'is [to be] followed by the decision to close down the base and return that territory to the Cubans,' a base that the United States 'really does not need for its security and defense.'"

Following Cuba's lead, liberal bloggers are clamoring that the base be abandoned. John Peeler in the *LA Progressive* claims our base is a "symbol of arrogant lawlessness" and is "a metaphor for Yankee imperialism," which "has outraged Latin Americans for over a century." On the MyDD blog, Charles Lemos argues that it is "time to unwind an empire the United States should have never acquired in the first place. Moreover, the lease of Guantánamo Bay is likely illegal under international law."

Such cliché claims are simply not true. Chavez, Morales, and Zelaya will not abandon their hatred of America if we appease the Castros by handing over our base. They will only be emboldened to demand that we further appease them as they continue to dismantle the rule of law in Venezuela and Bolivia and attempt to do so in Honduras. Nor is there any legitimate basis for claiming that the US base violates international law. America has scrupulously abided by its treaty with Cuba that was signed, on our part, by President Franklin Delano Roosevelt. As to charges about imperialism, the handful of Cubans currently on the base are those who worked there when Castro took over the island and, not surprisingly, do not want to go back, as well as those refugees that were able to dodge the bullets of Cuban frontier guards and swim to the base in a desperate attempt to gain their freedom.

As soon as the detainees make it to the continental United States, watch the liberal blogosphere buzz with claims of "people will like us more" if we leave and America is violating "international law" as the campaign to force the abandonment of GTMO heats up. Such charges are not true. But essentially the same assertions were not true with respect to the detainee issue either. They worked once, so the Castros and the left will use the same playbook again. For the security of the United States and for the benefit of the rest of the democracies in our hemisphere, let us hope that they do not. ∎

⇒ | ⇐

Observer Dispatches from Guantánamo

In April 2014, the Pacific Council was invited to send an observer to a week of Military Commission hearings in the case of *US v. Khalid Sheikh Mohammed, et al.* at Naval Station Guantánamo Bay, Cuba (GTMO). Khalid Sheikh Mohammed (KSM) is accused of masterminding the September 11 attacks on the World Trade Center and has been linked to many other attacks between 1993 and 2003. He is on trial with four other alleged co-conspirators.

The History

In order to provide context for these *Dispatches*, it is useful to consider the past use of military commissions, and particularly GTMO, by the United States. In what was essentially the first American use of the procedure, General George Washington established a court of inquiry to try Major John Andre, a British officer and suspected spy. Andre was captured wearing civilian clothes and carrying documents obtained from Benedict Arnold relating to the defense of West Point. He was tried and sentenced to death in substantially the same manner that the British had earlier dealt with the American officer and accused spy, Nathan Hale. Since that time, military commissions have been employed in almost

This article was originally published by the Pacific Council on International Policy, April 2014.

every American conflict, including the Mexican-American War (during which the term "military commission" was first used), the Civil War, the Spanish-American War, World War I, and World War II.

The US Supreme Court has upheld the constitutionality of military commissions on several occasions in various wars. In *Ex parte Quirin*, the court upheld the convictions and sentences of eight German saboteurs who landed in New York by German U-boat and were subsequently arrested wearing civilian clothes. They were tried and six of them were sentenced to death pursuant to an order issued on July 2, 1942, by President Franklin D. Roosevelt. President Roosevelt's order was very similar to President Bush's military order that established the military commissions following 9/11. In *Quirin*, the court held that unlawful combatants are "subject to trial and punishment by military tribunals for acts which render their belligerency unlawful." The court also held that the accused in military commissions are not entitled to the same constitutional safeguards afforded defendants in civilian courts: "Section 2 of Article III and the Fifth and Sixth Amendments cannot be taken to have extended the right to demand a jury to trials by military commissions, or to have required that offenses against the law of war not triable by jury at common law be tried only in the civil courts."

The current proceedings in GTMO are governed by the Military Commissions Act, as amended by the Military Commissions Act of 2009 (MCA). The MCA establishes jurisdiction over "alien unprivileged enemy belligerents" for violations of the law of war or the offenses specifically enumerated under the MCA. Notably, the MCA includes conspiracy charges, which international law does not recognize as a war crime. In January 2013, the Military Commission prosecution represented that it would dismiss the conspiracy charge against KSM, but soon after retracted that position. The MCA also sets forth certain procedural safeguards, which differ in some respects from the rights afforded to criminal defendants in federal court.

The Case

During the week of April 14, 2014, the Military Commission was set to continue pretrial hearings in *US v. Khalid Sheikh Mohammed, et al.* As widely reported, KSM is the alleged mastermind of the September 11 attacks on the United States. Charges against him and his four co-defendants, who were also allegedly involved in the September 11 attacks, include conspiracy, murder in violation of the law of war, attacking civilians, attacking civilian objects, intentionally causing serious bodily injury, destruction of property in violation of the law of war, terrorism, and material support of terrorism.

The United States captured the defendants in 2002 and 2003 and held them in secret detention facilities abroad. In 2008, they were transferred to the detention facilities at GTMO and the initial arraignment was conducted on June 5, 2008. Soon after President Obama took office in 2009, he issued an executive order to close the GTMO detention facility. Amid concerns about national security, Congress intervened. Using funding restrictions, they prohibited transferring the non-citizen Guantánamo detainees to the United States for prosecution (or any other purpose).

The current 9/11 proceedings began in May 2012 with a twelve-hour arraignment hearing of the five defendants. The Military Commission has conducted several rounds of pretrial hearings since then, most recently in December 2013.

Protection of the attorney-client privilege has been a hotly contested issue in the case. In January 2013, the defense counsel raised concerns about microphones disguised as smoke detectors located in rooms where counsel met with defendants. The judge, Army Colonel James Pohl, ordered prison officials to remove the microphones, "[t]he sooner the better." At the same hearing, the defense counsel questioned a military official about the seizure of confidential documents from the cells of three defendants, including KSM.

The trial is currently scheduled for early 2015, but there is real doubt that it will occur before 2016 or even 2017. After this week's proceedings, it is hard to see how Chief Prosecutor Army Brigadier General Mark Martins will maintain the schedule, absent additional and longer hearings at GTMO, prior to January 2015. Nevertheless, Martins expressed confidence that the trial schedule would remain in place.

April 12, 2014: Getting to Guantánamo Bay

The visit to GTMO begins at the "President's Airport," Andrews Air Force Base, located in suburban Maryland. Seating on the Delta charter flight is open but each group was asked to board and sit in groups. Media and NGO observers sat in the back, followed by the defense team, prosecution team, and the judge. The first-class cabin was reserved for the 9/11 victims' family members.

Traveling in the back with the media and NGO folks had the feel of a campaign plane or bus: lots of information, gossip, and theories floated through that part of the cabin. One defense-associated lawyer explained that if the case ever gets to trial, KSM would likely argue that he planned the attacks out of "necessity" to defend the Muslim *ummah* (people or community) from America, which had "attacked" them by establishing bases in Saudi Arabia, home of the Holy Places, and "abandoning" the people of Afghanistan after the Soviets left the country on February 15, 1989. Since the *ummah*, as represented by al-Qaeda, did not have an air force to attack the United States, it was forced to obtain one by hijacking civilian airliners. I mentioned that such an argument probably will not play well before a jury of American military officers. The response was a shrug.

We landed at Leeward Point Field and cleared the military equivalent of customs by showing our passports (no Cuba entry stamps) and our travel documents supplied by the Office of Military Commissions (OMC). This was my second visit to GTMO. While serving as co-chairman of the Public Private Partnership for Justice Reform in Afghanistan, I spent a day on base in 2009 viewing the Joint Task Force's detention facilities and receiving a briefing on detainee issues from the then-JTF commander. There is also a bit of family history at the base. My father deployed to the naval station as a young Marine Corps officer during the Cuban Missile Crisis.

In 2009, I observed the detention camps and, at the time, was impressed by the professional manner in which our young soldiers and sailors undertook the difficult custodial work with which they were charged. I also noted the humane and clean living, recreational, culinary, and medical facilities provided to the detainees. The International Committee of the Red Cross (ICRC) has routinely monitored the detention facilities since 2002 and recently completed its hundredth visit to GTMO. Not surprisingly, given the security surrounding the proceedings, the NGO observers on this visit are not permitted to visit the detention facilities, something that is not appreciated by several of the human rights organizations.

GTMO definitely has the feel of a naval facility. Each morning at 8:00, all activity comes to a halt for the National Anthem, which is played over the base's loud speakers. What makes GTMO really unique is that its surroundings transport you back half a century. The base architecture, paint scheme, and period buildings are similar to the old Canal Zone or the Presidio. Old pill boxes, naval gun emplacements, and ammunition bunkers dot the base and recall a time when it was a frontline base in the Cold War. The massive piers in the harbor once regularly hosted American battleships. Just off the piers are long rows of at least fifty pay phones. It is easy to imagine hundreds of sailors charging down the gangways to the phones to place collect calls to wives and girlfriends following a cruise. Like the machine gun nests, the pay phones now belong to another era.

The paint peels on old unused buildings throughout the base, which in many places are in a state of arrested decay. The Cuban Cultural Center, once home to the naval station's hundreds of Cuban employees, is empty. The last two Cubans, who enjoyed grandfathered jobs on the base, retired two years ago. They have been replaced by hundreds of Filipino workers (recalling earlier days in the US Navy). Jamaicans also make up a large component of the contractor force.

Housed within this cocoon of an aging imperial naval station are modern detention facilities and courtrooms. While only a few hundred miles from the continental United States, the base has an expeditionary atmosphere. The housing at Camp Justice consists of tents (thankfully, air conditioned due to the good work of Air Force engineers) and container-style units built on the runways of the old McCalla airfield. The courthouse is surrounded by rings of security with checkpoints, towers, chain link fencing, and concertina wire. Military Police (MPs) patrol with sidearms.

Morale is sustained in the "little America" base town by free admission to nightly first-run movies shown at a balmy outdoor theater. The GTMO Scuba shop is the best-stocked and friendliest dive shop I have ever visited. Scuba diving is the preferred hobby of the soldiers and sailors who come through GTMO on nine or twelve month rotations. Many arrive never having participated in the sport and leave as PADI-qualified dive masters or instructors. The packed dirt nine-hole golf course, where only the greens are watered, does not offer the same experience to golfers as the Caribbean does for the divers. It was, however, the site of a recent PGA morale-boosting tournament attended by several top professionals.

After checking into our tents, the defense lawyers, in a GTMO tradition, hosted the NGO observers for a backyard BBQ. The hospitality was kind and the informal briefings were generous. Eating hot dogs and drinking Coca-Cola on a hot Cuban night just miles away from the "cactus curtain" was interesting.

April 13, 2014: Hearings Begin

Sunday brunch with fellow NGO observers on the patio of the GTMO Officer's Club had an "old school" feel. In light of the location, there were, of course, several attempts at the famous Colonel Nathan Jessup line in *A Few Good Men*: "I eat breakfast 300 yards from 4,000 Cubans who are trained to kill me, so don't think for one second that you can come down here, flash a badge, and make me nervous."

In the overseas equivalent of a Hollywood star sighting, we watched from our table as legendary war photographer James Nachtwey shot photos of Canal Plus White House correspondent Laura Haim, as she in turn interviewed several 9/11 family members. Several of us had the opportunity to talk with Nachtwey, who was the subject of the 2001 award-winning documentary *War Photographer*, over dinner later in the week. He was generous with his time and perceptive in his observations although his politics are far from mine.

One of the highlights of visits to overseas military bases for me is the ability to attend worship services with our soldiers, sailors, airmen, Marines, and Coast Guardsmen. Given how little free time our deployed troops often have, it is heartwarming to see them enjoy the fellowship and spirit that is present at these services. There is a mixing of branches and ranks in such a setting that is unique within the military.

We were at the naval station during the Christian Holy Week as well as the Jewish Passover holidays. Visitors to GTMO were welcomed by the chaplain's column in the JTF's weekly newsletter. The chaplain, Commander Stephen A. Gammon, noted the religious significance of the week and provided information on where different denominations would hold their services.

GTMO is home to a beautiful turn-of-the-century chapel. It is also home to a number of Roman Catholic roadside shrines built by Cuban base employees when they were the mainstay of the civilian work force. It was hard not to contrast the infrastructure for free worship at GTMO with the situation just over the "cactus curtain" in Cuba, where the US Department of State's annual International Religious Freedom Report states: "[m]any [clergy] feared that direct or indirect criticism of the government could result in government reprisals...or other measures that could stymie the growth of their organizations."

April 14, 2014: Conflict of Interest

Notwithstanding GTMO's remote location and status as a naval station located on a foreign island, where only military personnel and approved visitors are permitted, the security around the Military Commission court facilities is a ring of steel. Armed MPs check IDs at multiple points. We pass through magnetometers. Military personnel escort the 9/11 families, NGO observers, and the media at all times. No cameras, phones, laptops, or electronic devices of any kind are allowed within the premises. Special software and sensors can detect them and will alert security personnel to the offending device (which occurred once).

The 9/11 families, the NGO observers, and the media share the gallery at the back of the courtroom. The media contingent included the *Guardian*'s Spencer Ackerman, Dave Cullen, writing a freelance piece for the *New Republic*, French war correspondent Laura Haim, James Nachtwey, a Dutch reporter on assignment and the dean of the GTMO press corps, and the *Miami Herald*'s Carol Rosenberg. As no cameras are allowed in the courtroom, talented courtroom artist Janet Hamlin busily sketched pictures of the participants in the proceedings.

The courtroom follows the traditional layout with a bench, witness, and jury boxes and a well where stenographers and clerks work. The five defendants sit at tables in a row, one behind the other, with their four- to six-person legal teams composed of uniformed Judge Advocate General (JAG) lawyers and learned civilian counsel, several of whom are famous for their past death penalty cases.

The prosecution team is an interagency affair led by General Martins and his JAG lawyers and supplemented by Department of Justice prosecutors. They sit in rows of desks facing the bench with the jury box to their right.

KSM sits to the far left of his table, as do all defendants. He was not apparently restrained from our vantage point but could have been shackled. He is pudgy and has a bushy red beard that is reportedly dyed using fruit juice and berries from his meals. Each day he wore a white turban and *shalwar kameez* or *dishdasha* (it was hard to tell which as he sat during our time in court) covered by an Army woodlands-style battle dress field jacket.

Immediately behind him sat Walid bin Attash, a Yemeni. Bin Attash was attired the same as KSM but wore a 1990s desert-style battle dress field jacket. Ramzi bin al-Shibh, another Yemeni, wore the same dress as bin Attash. Ali Abdul Aziz Ali (aka Amar al-Baluchi) from Pakistan wore a white *thobe* and red-and-white-checkered headdress like the one that Yasser Arafat made famous. Mustafa al-Hawsawi, a Saudi, wore a white *dishdasha* and white turban.

Each of the defendants brought his own prayer rug and large plastic box containing his legal papers with him.

Approximately twenty-five Army MPs provided security within the courtroom. Most stood along the wall closest to the defendants' seats. All had "Internal Security" in place of name tags on their uniforms. This is standard practice for personnel at the camps, who still fear al-Qaeda reprisals on themselves or their families if associates of the detainees were to discover their identities. When I asked one soldier where he was from, he politely declined to tell me—a first in my many years of interactions with our soldiers, who usually enjoy talking about home. They know the potential consequences, even in the United States, of being on an al-Qaeda hit list.

The first day of court ended in dramatic fashion just thirty-six minutes into the proceedings. My fellow NGO observer, Brett Max Kaufman, a young ACLU fellow and former Second Circuit clerk, posted the following accurate summary of events on his blog:

> Just minutes after Army Col. James Pohl called the courtroom roll, defense lawyers revealed that, hours earlier, they had filed an emergency motion seeking to stop this week's proceedings and asking the court to investigate yet another instance of alleged government meddling with defense counsel in this death penalty case. This time, said James Harrington—lead counsel for bin al-Shibh—two FBI agents visited the Defense Security Officer assigned to bin al-Shibh's defense team on the morning of Sunday, April 6... Defense attorneys raised a related concern: Have other members of defense staffs been approached—and

gagged from ever saying so? Today in court—before a stunned gallery of journalists and NGO observers—the defense lawyers asked Judge Pohl a simple question: How can they advise their clients on any issue if they are uncertain whether serious conflicts of interests (such as an FBI investigation of the lawyers) might prevent them from giving those clients unbiased, confidential advice?

April 15–16, 2014: Recess

Judge Pohl ruled on what had been expected to be the primary issue for the week's hearing: whether alleged 9/11 co-conspirator bin al-Shibh is competent to stand trial. Since the defense is not disputing bin al-Shibh's competence, the judge held that the presumption of competence meant that the hearings could proceed until someone proved the Yemeni defendant was incompetent.

The FBI's investigation of the defense team, however, remained front and center in the brief proceedings. Kaufman, again, captured the defense position and Judge Pohl's concern in his blog post:

> Defense lawyers have asked for an independent inquiry by the military commission into the circumstances of the FBI investigation, which reportedly centers on the publication early this year of a series of letters written by 9/11 defendant Khalid Sheikh Mohammed. They argue that only after the court examines the facts surrounding the DSO interview—and any other FBI contact with members of the defense teams—can they determine whether they are faced with a conflict of interest that would undermine the effective representation of their clients.

Over concerns raised by the DOJ's lead counsel, but not General Martins, Judge Pohl did order all members of the five defense teams to inform their lead counsel if any of them had been contacted by the FBI.

With the military commission in recess for the day while the defense prepared discovery requests relating to the FBI investigation, 9/11 family member frustration with the slow proceedings boiled over. It was reported within Camp Justice that many of the family members were blaming the defense teams, the NGOs, and the FBI for the delays in the proceedings.

General Martins hosted a morning meeting with the NGOs for an "off the record" question-and-answer session. He fielded tough questions from the human rights lawyers and law student observers. His answers were direct and reasonable. He was modest and engaging. While he may not have won many converts among those who oppose the military commission process, I believe that he earned their respect based on his integrity and openness.

April 17–18, 2014: Full Circle

It is an odd experience to sit in a civilized courtroom setting and observe the behavior of a man—KSM—who planned the mass murder of three thousand Americans. My thoughts turned to the famous black-and-white stills of the courtroom at Nuremberg where justice was dispensed to Nazi war criminals.

The military commission session today was basically a short status conference in which Judge Pohl attempted to determine a way forward. After a total of just over three hours in court over the course of four days, the military commission proceedings ended just where they had started on Monday—centered on the alleged FBI investigation into KSM's defense team.

Prior to departing GTMO, General Martins issued a brief statement saying:

> Of course, our hearts go out to the family members of those who were killed on 9/11, and we can certainly understand their frustration. Still, we are determined to move forward under the supervision of the Judge. When each of us was assigned to this important mission, we were prepared for a marathon. We remain so.

Final Thoughts

America still produces heroes—and more often than not they can be found in our armed forces. It is our young soldiers, sailors, airmen, Marines, and Coast Guardsmen, however, that are most inspiring. Most of the uniformed personnel running our military are in their late teens and early twenties. They are professional, courteous, and courageous. They are called upon to exercise judgment well beyond their years. America can be proud of her troops, and that goes for those involved in the military commission proceedings as well.

General Mark Martins looks the part of the Chief Prosecutor. He walks the walk. A warrior with a Ranger tab and a Harvard law degree, he passed up his most recent promotion board and a sure second star to stay in his current role to "get the job done" for the American people and the 9/11 families. Hopefully, when that happens, the Army will reward General Martins with the additional star he deserves and keep him leading our troops.

Major Jason Wright is an impressive young Army officer with enough medals and ribbons to show that the Army believes the same. He is assigned to the KSM defense team. Under other circumstances, I have no doubt that Major Wright would be fully engaged in any effort to "find, fix, and finish" KSM. But as his assigned defense lawyer, he resigned his active duty Army commission rather than leave the defense team and report to the JAG Advanced School, a required step to promotion. Major Wright believes that his ethical duties as a lawyer require him not to abandon his client mid-case. He announced the decision to the court without complaint about his orders or a request for the judge's intervention. It was a gutsy move based on principle.

America is defined by its commitment to the rule of law. Its written constitution remains the model document for almost all the nations of the world—whether they abide by the principles of liberty enshrined in the document or not. It is not surprising, therefore, that the press, many of the NGO observers, law professors, and others of goodwill are deeply concerned with the rights provided to the accused war criminals in these proceedings. This is a badge of honor for our country, the very foundations of which were built on the ideals of an adversarial system, right to counsel, trial by jury (including in a military commission), and a neutral judge to preside over criminal proceedings. Judge Pohl's careful handling of the FBI investigation and attention to the defendants' attorney-client privilege are in the best traditions of American jurisprudence.

Too often the rights of victims of crime—in this case, mass murder in a heinous act of terrorism—are forgotten. The United States military has not forgotten the 9/11 families. Their presence at the proceedings is a poignant reminder to all of us that thousands of families are still suffering the consequences of the attack. On the ferry ride across the harbor to catch our plane home, one father, accompanied by his eldest son, shared with me the story of the loss of his son.

The young man was a twenty-six-year-old commodities trader who was killed on impact when one of the hijacked American Airlines jets slammed into his office in the Twin Towers. The father spoke with genuine pride in his son, who had moved to New York, grown to love the city, and found success and reward in his young career. He told me of his son's soccer games as a kid and how his son always sought out risks. He talked about his son's friends, who now have families of their own. Despite the passage of years, this dad was not over—and never will get over—the senseless murder of his son.

The Military Commission cannot bring back his son or the other 9/11 family members' lost loved ones. It can—and, based on my observations, likely will—bring to justice the perpetrators of the 9/11 atrocity in a manner that is consistent with our nation's enduring commitment to the rule of law. ■

SECTION 5

Obama White House Falsely Blames Ambassador Patterson for Morsi Mess

In Josh Rogin's and Eli Lake's *Daily Beast* column this week, current and former "Obama administration officials" anonymously attempt to shift blame for President Obama's failed engagement with Egypt's Muslim Brotherhood to career foreign service officer and current US Ambassador to Egypt, Anne Patterson.

While such spin from the White House and its political allies is not surprising, given America's rudderless Middle East policy, the Obama administration's latest effort is not just a red herring—it is disrespectful to one of our nation's finest diplomats.

I personally saw Ambassador Patterson's commitment to US national security policy at the UN, where she served as a deputy and acting Chief of Mission during the Bush administration.

Patterson was relentless in standing up to America's adversaries at Turtle Bay and took on anyone who stood in the way of America's priorities.

Such conduct was to be expected from Patterson, who had previously been America's Ambassador to Colombia, during which time she was under constant threat from drug lords and leftist guerrillas.

In subsequent assignments, Patterson served as Assistant Secretary of State for International Narcotics and Law Enforcement, where she ran

This article was originally published on *FoxNews.com*, July 11, 2013.2014.

America's efforts to eradicate Afghanistan's poppy plantations and cut off the Taliban's narco-profits, and as Ambassador to Pakistan during the past several years in which a fragile Pakistan also changed leadership.

Patterson is no neophyte. She certainly understands that it is not in America's interest to have an Islamist party in charge of Egypt.

I am sure she would have been happier if Washington had done more to support the secularists, moderate Muslims, and Christians in Egypt, who longed for a rule-of-law-based society after the fall of US ally Hosni Mubarak. But that was not the administration's policy in Egypt or in the region.

When the Green Revolution was unfolding on the streets of Tehran, there was silence from the White House and the mullahs tightened their grip in Iran.

When the moderate opposition to Assad was desperate for our support in Syria, little was forthcoming from this administration. Moderates were sidelined there as they were in Egypt.

Once the Muslim Brotherhood gained power in Cairo, Patterson, as the implementer of the White House's foreign policy, had to deal with that reality.

The US ambassador is the president's representative in a foreign land. It is the president's policy that our ambassadors implement. It was President Obama's demand that Patterson engage the Muslim Brotherhood. For administration staffers to now suggest that it was Patterson's policy is ridiculous.

No one should be surprised by the course this administration chose. Then-Senator Obama made it clear in his 2008 debate clash with Hillary Clinton that he believes America "has to talk to its enemies." Indeed, at the same time that the administration was engaging the Muslim Brotherhood in Cairo, it was setting up peace talks with the Taliban in Qatar, to the apparent chagrin of our ally President Hamid Karzai in Kabul.

Now that a large swath of the Egyptian people, backed by the Army, has removed President Morsi and the Muslim Brotherhood from office, unnamed administration officials believe that the Arkansas-born Patterson, who has excelled under presidents from both political parties and is respected on both sides of the aisle, should be the scapegoat. That cannot be allowed to happen. ■

≡ | ⇐

Is the Benghazi Attack Obama's Madrid Train Bombings?

O n March 11, 2004, bombs ripped through Madrid's commuter train system, killing 191 people and wounding an additional 1,800. The terrorist attack took place three days before Spain's general election and completely turned it upside down. The ruling People's Party, led by then-Spanish Prime Minister José María Aznar, chose to cast blame on Spain's Basque separatist organization ETA, while the Socialist opposition pointed to al-Qaeda as the culprit.

By blaming ETA, Aznar's camp hoped to curry votes by drawing attention to their leader's tough campaign against the Spanish terror organization. The Socialists, on the other hand, hoped voters would hold Aznar responsible for having incited Islamic extremists by his support of America's war in Iraq, which was exceedingly unpopular in Spain.

In the end, the Socialists won. Not only were they correct in blaming al-Qaeda, they were also able to capitalize on a major mistake by Aznar's team—one almost identical to the mistake being carried out by Team Obama in the wake of the deadly Benghazi attack.

Within hours of the bombings in Madrid, Aznar's foreign minister sent a memo to Spain's ambassadors instructing them to blame ETA for the attack. And despite police rounding up a number of Moroccan-born suspects the evening before the election, Spain's interior minister

This article was originally published on *PJMedia.com*, October 14, 2012.

115

continued to claim that the police investigation was focused on ETA. The Spanish government wasn't fooling anyone, especially its citizens. They knew who was behind the bombings. The ruling party's less-than-credible insistence that ETA was responsible led enough voters to switch their support away from Aznar—who up to that point had been a sure thing—and over to his Socialist challenger, who would go on to a stunning come-from-behind victory and eventually usher in drastic changes in Spain's domestic and foreign policy.

While not of the same magnitude in loss of life as the Madrid bombings, the Benghazi attack of September 11, 2012, saw Ambassador J. Christopher Stevens and three of his colleagues (Sean Smith, Tyrone Woods, and Glen Doherty) murdered and the American consulate set aflame. Having committed to a political calculation, the Obama administration set off in the wake of those attacks in much the same fashion as the doomed Aznar administration did.

Five days later, and despite clear evidence that there was, in fact, no mob, but instead a well-planned and executed terrorist attack, the Obama administration dispatched UN Ambassador Susan Rice to appear on the Sunday talk shows to give the White House's version of events.

Ambassador Rice was an interesting choice of spokesperson, which brings to mind the question: Why wasn't Secretary of State Clinton available? Was she perhaps not willing to carry the administration's water?

Ambassador Rice stated on CBS's *Face the Nation*:

> Based on the best information we have to date…it began spontaneously in Benghazi as a reaction to what had transpired some hours earlier in Cairo, where, of course, as you know, there was a violent protest outside of our embassy sparked by this hateful video. But soon after that spontaneous protest began outside of our consulate in Benghazi we believe that it looks like extremist elements, individuals, joined in that effort with heavy weapons of the sort that are, unfortunately, readily now available in Libya post-revolution. And that it spun from there into something much, much more violent. We do not have information at present that leads us to conclude that this was premeditated or preplanned.

Three days later, however, in sworn testimony before the Senate Homeland Security and Governmental Affairs Committee, Matthew

Olsen, the director of the National Counterterrorism Center, testified: "Yes, they were killed in the course of a terrorist attack on our embassy. We are looking at indications that individuals involved in the attack may have had connections to al-Qaeda or al-Qaeda's affiliates; in particular, al-Qaeda in the Islamic Maghreb."

Nevertheless, ignoring Olsen's testimony and the mounting evidence that Benghazi constituted a coordinated terrorist attack on an American diplomatic facility, the next day, at the Univision Town Hall, President Obama again raised the specter of a protest over the offensive video being to blame for the murders of Ambassador Stevens and his colleagues:

> Well, we're still doing an investigation, and there are going to be differ-
> ent circumstances in different countries. And so I don't want to speak
> to something until we have all the information. What we do know is
> that the natural protests that arose because of the outrage over the video
> were used as an excuse by extremists to see if they can also directly
> harm US interests.

Based on extensive reporting by CNN, the *Wall Street Journal*, and Fox News, there is no longer any doubt that Benghazi was a sophisticated and pre-planned terrorist attack against the United States. Indeed, the Obama administration very likely knew this at a much earlier stage than it has admitted.

In the face of congressional hearings, the State Department asserts that it never concluded the consulate attack in Benghazi arose from pro-tests over the video. When asked about the Obama administration's initial explanation linking the attacks in Benghazi to protests over the video, a State Department official said, "That was not our conclusion"—the impli-cation being that those talking points had come from the White House.

The *Washington Post*'s Glenn Kessler wrote that "for political reasons, it certainly was in the White House's interests to not portray the attack as a terrorist incident, especially one that took place on the anniversary of the September 11 attacks. Instead the administration kept the focus on what was ultimately a red herring—anger in the Arab world over anti-Muslim video posted on YouTube." The political reasons for the Obama administration's portrayal of the attack arise from the fact that Benghazi fundamentally undermines White House claims that "leading from behind" resulted in success in Libya, that extremely conciliatory gestures to the Muslim world would defuse Islamic extremism, that the global war on terror is over and al-Qaeda defeated with the killing of Osama bin Laden, and that the administration had given proper consideration to the safety of American diplomats operating in Libya.

On Monday, in his speech at the Virginia Military Institute, Governor Romney gave voice to what Americans already knew to be true:

> The attack on our consulate in Benghazi on September 11, 2012, was likely the work of forces affiliated with those that attacked our homeland on September 11, 2001. This latest assault cannot be blamed on a reprehensible video insulting Islam, despite the administration's attempts to convince us of that for so long. No, as the administration has finally conceded, these attacks were the deliberate work of terrorists who use violence to impose their dark ideology on others, especially women and girls; who are fighting to control much of the Middle East today; and who seek to wage perpetual war on the West.

Just as Spanish voters figured out in the mere three days between the Madrid bombings and the election (despite their government's effort to point the finger at ETA) that al-Qaeda was responsible, American voters are determining, as congressional hearings unfold and common-sense analysis takes over, that the Benghazi murders were a coordinated and pre-planned attack on America—not spontaneous mob violence arising from an offensive video, a claim the administration has clung to for so long.

In less than thirty days, we will know if the Obama administration will pay a price at the polls for its handling of Benghazi and its aftermath, just as the Spanish government did for Madrid. ■

The Good, the Bad, and the Ugly in Afghanistan
Why Justice Sector Reform Matters

In January, I traveled to Afghanistan. It was my first visit since February of 2008. Importantly, there is good news from Kabul. Commerce is flourishing. Having lived along the crossroads of civilizations for thousands of years, Afghans are natural-born traders and shopkeepers. Unlike the situation three years ago, the streets are clogged with traffic, the sidewalks are packed with vendors of all manner of goods, and stores and restaurants line the streets. The Western-oriented hotels are able to host conferences and upscale wedding halls dot the city. Construction and rebuilding is evident throughout Kabul.

With the surge reaching critical mass, General David Petraeus and the ISAF forces are effectively implementing his counterinsurgency strategy designed to protect the population, eliminate terrorist networks, defeat the insurgents, and train competent, trustworthy, and professional Afghan security forces. They are indeed driving the Taliban out of their strongholds and standing up the Afghan National Army. Counterterrorism missions—most notably, the recent operation that eliminated Osama bin Laden—are sapping the strength and diminishing the leadership capacity of al-Qaeda in the region.

American combat victories against the Taliban and al-Qaeda, however, will not alone be sufficient to secure a stable Afghanistan. General

This article was originally published in the *Diplomatic Courier*, June 6, 2011.

Petraeus has identified "ineffective governance" and the "unwillingness to pursue political inclusion" by the Afghan government, as "strategic risks" to ISAF's ability to win the war. On this front, the news is not so good.

At every turn, ordinary Afghans complain about the rampant corruption in their land. American and allied diplomats confirm that the problems are systemic and go to the top. Afghan policemen arrest corrupt officials and narco-traffickers only to see them walk free when prosecutors, under pressure from senior officials, decline to pursue the cases. Afghan prosecutors are paid so little that they readily admit to taking bribes. Judges who take a hard line against corrupt officials have been driven from the bench by higher-ups, arrested, or simply murdered. Even when the guilty are convicted, the well connected are often pardoned. The effect of such corruption undermines the professional justice sector officials that we are spending hundreds of millions dollars to train and equip. It also means that it is almost impossible to roll out a rule-of-law-based society in the areas newly liberated from the Taliban by coalition forces.

As demonstrated by President Karzai's refusal in January to seat the elected Parliament, which he supposedly felt was insufficiently Pashtun, ethnic and tribal divisions continue to wrack Afghanistan. The fact that the Taliban draws its support primarily from the Pashtun belt that runs through Afghanistan and Pakistan exacerbates the ethic differences in the country. The Taliban's cross-border tribal ties to Pakistan is one of the factors that allows for sanctuaries to exist for the insurgents, who can retreat beyond the reach of American forces.

Establishing a rule-of-law-based society in Afghanistan is difficult in large part because it has been denied to the people of Afghanistan for over forty years by what Winston Churchill called the two "gaunt marauders, war and tyranny." In some academic or political circles, phrases such as the "rule of law" or "liberty" are sometimes labeled "Western constructs" that may not be suitable for the people of Afghanistan. Based on my experience, I strongly disagree.

In his July 17, 2003, address to a joint session of Congress, Prime Minister Tony Blair made an eloquent case for liberty and the rule of law:

> There is a myth that though we love freedom, others don't; that our attachment to freedom is a product of our culture; that freedom, democracy, human rights, the rule of law are American values or

Western values; that Afghan women were content under the lash of the Taliban; that Saddam was beloved by his people; that Milosevic was Serbia's savior. Members of Congress, ours are not Western values. They are the universal values of the human spirit. And anywhere, anytime, ordinary people are given the chance to choose, the choice is the same: Freedom, not tyranny; democracy, not dictatorship; the rule of law, not the rule of the secret police.

As we engage in justice sector reform efforts based on the rule of law in Afghanistan (and other post-conflict states), it is critical that we do not accept the myth that what we are promoting amounts to some type of Western cultural imperialism. Unfortunately, it is possible for even dedicated lawyers to fall into that trap. Let me illustrate the point with some lessons I have learned in working with the Department of State, federal judiciary, academia, and the private bar in a unique partnership that was developed to promote the rule of law in Afghanistan.

Secretary of State Condoleezza Rice launched the Public-Private Partnership for Justice Reform in Afghanistan in December 2007. In 2009, we hosted a group of Afghan female judges, prosecutors, and defense lawyers for a training program in Southern California. To give the Afghans a break from their studies, we arranged for a Sunday outing to the Getty Museum and the Santa Monica Pier. We assumed that our guests would be pleased to receive a private tour of the famous Getty Villa and its world-class collection of Greek and Roman sculptures and art. We did not foresee how they might react when confronted with realistic portrayals of the ancients in all their glory. Our guests were polite but did avert their eyes from the sculptures.

There is perhaps no venue this side of the *Star Wars* bar that is more interesting than the Santa Monica Pier. When we arrived, there was a Code Pink protest against the war in Afghanistan underway; scores of white crosses with the names of fallen soldiers and marines had been planted on the beach. On the other side of the pier, beach volleyball games were in full swing. The demographically diverse crowd on the pier was dressed for a hot day at the beach. Our Afghan colleagues pulled their scarves around their cheeks and tightened their shawls around their shoulders. They were anxious. Fortunately, we passed the soft-serve ice cream stand. The ladies had never tasted ice cream and eyed the line. A colleague of mine, US District Judge Stephen Larson, jumped into action and bought twenty chocolate-dipped vanilla cones for our guests. They were thrilled and began to relax. Emboldened, several of the Afghan lawyers pointed to the Ferris wheel and other carnival rides and gave them a shot.

On the way home, they could not stop talking about the day. What amazed these women was that so many diverse people could mingle in a small public area—engage in protests, sports, shopping, and recreation—and do so in a peaceful fashion. They commented on the fact that they did not see any police presence. Similarly, the fact that a collection of priceless art could be maintained at the Getty without tanks protecting it was an eye-opener. Far from our creating a politically incorrect incident, the day had taught the Afghans, on a profound level, that the rule of law, when ingrained in a culture, is precious. They experienced the blessings of liberty on that Sunday in Santa Monica in a way that we could not have conveyed in a classroom.

Such experiences have convinced me that rule of law and liberty are universal values that Afghans or Iraqis or Syrians or others desire just as much as we desire them in America, the United Kingdom, or the West. We engage in justice sector reform efforts because it is the right thing to do—but also because it is in our national interest. The spread of freedom and the rule of law are our best defense against tyranny and war.

It is, therefore, not surprising that General David Petraeus is a strong proponent of justice sector reform and rule of law programs in Afghanistan. General Petraeus understands that he needs to be able to "hand off" newly liberated areas to an Afghan police force, Attorney General's office, judiciary, and defense bar, which are fair and can deal with crime, terrorism, family law, and commercial disputes in a civil, not military, framework. If he is unable to do so, the success of the American surge could be in vain.

The path forward will not be easy for Afghanistan or the coalition. In February, a suicide bomber walked into a supermarket in the upscale Wazir Akbar Khan district of Kabul and detonated his bomb next to a family of six. The entire family was wiped out. The father was prominent Afghan physician Masood Yama. The mother was Kabul University law professor and women's rights activist Hameeda Barmaki. The four children were under fourteen years old. While the family was not the specific target, civilized society was. This family could have easily made a comfortable living abroad. Dr. Yama and Professor Barmaki, however, chose to return to Kabul after their overseas studies to rebuild their country. They are just the type of people that Afghanistan cannot afford to lose.

The Public-Private Partnership for Justice Reform in Afghanistan has a personal connection to the victims. Professor Barmaki's brother is currently studying to receive his LLM degree at George Washington University with a scholarship from the Partnership. After learning of his sister's death, he decided to continue his studies here and will return home to Afghanistan this summer. I applaud his courage and commitment to his country. Even in the face of such a terrible tragedy, there remains hope for a rule-of-law-based society in Afghanistan. ∎

≡ | ≋

Liberty and the Rule of Law are Universal Values

It is very special for me to return to Boalt Hall. I knew Stefan Riesenfeld and had the good fortune to be one of his students. He was a great man and a remarkable scholar of the law. I am both honored and humbled to be associated with his legacy and to have been asked by the *Berkeley Journal of International Law* to speak here today. Professor Riesenfeld's impact on Boalt Hall continues through the scholarship and teaching of Professors David Caron and Richard Buxbaum, both past recipients of the Stefan A. Riesenfeld Memorial Award.

I have been privileged to work with several of our panelists, including Dean Hiram Chodosh and Professor Michael Newton, in rule of law and justice sector reform projects both in government and in the private sector. The reputations of our other panelists are well established. Given what I know of your contributions in the field of international law, it is somewhat awkward for me to be at the podium to receive this prestigious award and not in the audience, honoring any of you. I accept it on behalf of the men and women who are working so hard to establish the rule of law on the front lines in Afghanistan—American JAG officers, diplomats, DOJ lawyers, and volunteers, as well as our Afghan colleagues who serve as prosecutors, judges, and defense lawyers.

This essay was adapted from the keynote address at the Stephen A. Riesenfeld Symposium at the University of California Berkeley School of Law, March 31, 2015.

Whether our work was assisting in justice sector reform in Afghanistan, advising governments on humanitarian law obligations in fighting insurgents and pirates in Africa, or resolving state claims against Iraq following the first Gulf War, our goal has remained the same: to promote the rule of law and liberty in states that have not enjoyed such blessings as a result of what Winston Churchill called the "two gaunt marauders, war and tyranny." I know that in some academic or political circles, phrases such as the "rule of law" or "blessings of liberty" are sometimes derisively considered to be "Western constructs." I submit that based on my experience, such principles are the bedrock upon which sustainable justice sector reform initiatives in post-conflict states are built anywhere in the world.

As we engage in justice sector reform efforts based on the rule of law and liberty, it is critical that we do not accept the myth that what we are promoting amounts to some type of Western cultural imperialism. Unfortunately, it is possible for even dedicated lawyers to fall into that trap. Let me illustrate the point with some lessons that I have learned in working with the Department of State, federal judiciary, academia, and the private bar in a unique partnership that was developed to promote the rule of law in Afghanistan.

Secretary of State Condoleezza Rice launched the Public-Private Partnership for Justice Reform in Afghanistan in December of 2007. I was asked to serve as the private sector co-chairman. One of our colleagues here today, Dean Hiram Chodosh, was among the founding members of the Partnership's executive committee. Secretary Rice's goal for the Partnership was to marshal the expertise of American lawyers, law school professors, and judges to assist Afghan lawyers to "build and reform democratic and independent institutions in their country." We wanted a Partnership that would focus on low-cost and high-impact projects that would fill in gaps in US rule of law aid to the country. To that end, among other initiatives, we have held several training sessions in the United States for Afghan prosecutors, women judges, and defense lawyers.

During one of the training sessions for Afghan defense lawyers last year, the State Department hosted a roundtable event, so that the staff of the then-AfPak Envoy, the late Ambassador Richard Holbrooke, could discuss rule of law issues with the visiting delegation. During the meeting, one of our Foreign Service Officers made a statement about how she felt it was important for America to respect Afghan culture and that the United States should begin to channel rule of law funds to the informal justice sector, specifically to the *shuras* and *jirgas*, or tribal councils.

Several of the Afghan women lawyers were visibly upset and one spoke up. This Afghan lawyer explained in no uncertain terms that women are not allowed to participate in *jirgas*. They are not allowed to defend themselves. Women lawyers are not permitted to represent clients in the proceedings. Female witnesses are prohibited from testifying. At best, a woman facing a civil claim or criminal charge in a *jirga* can have a male relative speak on her behalf while she waits outside. This Afghan lawyer made it clear that Afghan women and many Afghan men did not like the *jirgas* for the reason that women were denied their most basic rights under that system.

Clearly, this brave woman, who had won the right to attend law school and practice her profession as the result of the Coalition liberating Afghanistan from the Taliban, was surprised that an American colleague would suggest that the *jirga* system was best for Afghans. I do not blame the Foreign Service Officer who made the comment. We are faced with difficult circumstances in Afghanistan. We need to speed the transition there and are looking for ways to encourage greater responsibility in self governance by the Afghans. Though well-intentioned, she had bought into the myth that Afghans do not want the same basic human rights that we take for granted. We must be sensitive to local cultures and traditions when working overseas, especially in post-conflict states where tensions can run high. Such sensitivity or even humility, however, should not lead us to abandon the core principles that underlie the rule of law and our duty as lawyers when assisting others to build institutions of justice.

While our core principles should not change when we engage in justice sector reform efforts abroad, we do need to be respectful of how other societies and cultures implement them. As a lawyer in private practice, I handle cases in many jurisdictions. I can tell you that practicing in Cook County's trial courts is very different than arguing a case in the Ninth Circuit Court of Appeals. The frenetic Chicago trial courts seem to be a world away from the quiet, solemn federal circuit court houses in Pasadena or over in San Francisco. Nevertheless, American justice is dispensed fairly in both locales.

Similarly, justice can be fairly dispensed in humble circumstances even in post-conflict states. Several years ago, US District Judge Stephen Larson, Ambassador Pierre-Richard Prosper, and I were asked to observe the proceedings of an *Inkiko Gacaca,* or Grass Court, in a small village north of Kigali in Rwanda. As all of you know, Rwanda experienced a horrific genocide in 1994 when nearly one million people were slaughtered in one hundred days. The international community responded by creating a special criminal tribunal in Arusha. That court deals with high-level perpetrators of genocide. The Rwandans were left to deal with the rank-and-file killers and those who had aided and abetted them. For the lower-level culprits, a system of village courts was instituted. The number of defendants going through the system was staggering; estimates ranged as high as one hundred thousand people. The only way to dispense justice in a timely fashion was to do so through an informal system.

The *Inkiko Gacaca* we attended was one of four courts in session on a large soccer field that day. The local judges, elected by their fellow villagers, had received some training but were not lawyers. They sat at wooden tables facing the accused and the prosecutor. Villagers and witnesses sat or stood on the grass to watch the trials. Herders with their cattle would wander through the field from time to time, causing the courts to take short recesses as the cows passed through.

At the outset of the case, the prosecutor read the charges. The defendant, a former teacher, spoke up that he was the wrong guy and was not present in the village when the alleged crime occurred. He pointed the finger at his successor. The prosecutor, in turn, handed the court a list of teachers assigned to the village during the relevant time that contained the defendant's name. The defendant asked where the list came from and disputed whether it was the original record from the school.

A witness testified that he had heard from another person that the defendant was in the village when the alleged offense took place. The defendant asked why the person who claimed that the defendant was in the village the day of the offense was not present to be questioned at trial. The defendant voluntarily told his side of the story. Those attending the trial were then allowed to ask questions of the prosecutor, defendant, and court. The judges decided to deliberate and announce their ruling at later time. If found guilty, the defendant would likely be sentenced to some form of community service to improve the lives of the people hurt by the genocide. (Without labeling them as such, an alibi defense was raised and impeached. Objections based on best evidence and hearsay were posed. Witnesses were cross-examined and the judges deliberated.)

In light of the emotional nature of the charges and the location of the proceeding, the decorum with which the judges, prosecutor, accused, and audience conducted themselves was admirable. The fact that the process was designed not just to punish offenders but also to reconcile communities clearly had something to do with the attitude of the participants. There was a majesty in that grass court that I would equate with any court in which I have practiced. To be sure, it was not derived from the physical infrastructure of the facilities. It emanated from the simple fact that the court followed the principles of fairness that underlie the concept we refer to as the rule of law. Although the rules, environment, and culture of the court were unfamiliar to us, we were comfortable in that court as lawyers because the principles of justice being implemented were very familiar to us.

Such experiences have convinced me that rule of law and liberty are universal values. Afghans, Rwandans, Iraqis, and others desire them as much as we desire them in America, the United Kingdom, or the West. Those of us who work in the field seek to establish fair justice sectors in post-conflict states because it is the compassionate and right thing to do for our global neighbors. But there is another reason to be engaged in this cause: our national interests depend upon such work. The spread of freedom is our best defense against tyranny and war.

It is not just economists and lawyers who recognize the positive national security implications arising from the firm establishment of the rule of law in a nation. I was in Kabul in January and was briefed on the progress of the surge. The battlefield news was good. Our soldiers, sailors, airmen, Marines, and Coast Guardsmen are clearing the Taliban from entire provinces. Roads that had previously gone unused are now humming with commerce—even in Helmand and Kandahar. But General Petraeus identified in his war plans "ineffective governance and the unwillingness to pursue political inclusion by the Afghan government" (read: rule of law) as being strategic risks to ISAF's ability to win the war. Accordingly, it is General Petraeus who is one of the biggest proponents of justice sector reform and rule of law programs in Afghanistan. He needs to be able to "hand off" newly liberated areas to an Afghan police force, Attorney General's office, judiciary, and defense bar, which are fair and can deal with crime, terrorism, family law, and commercial disputes in a civil, not military, framework. Unfortunately, as we know, the news is very mixed on this front and, thus, America continues its efforts to bolster the justice sector and fight corruption in Afghanistan.

I have spoken at some length today about my belief that the rule of law and the blessings of liberty are rights that all men and women deserve. As we work to assist those people around the world who are seeking to rebuild, strengthen, and reform their justice sectors, we must promote the rule of law and liberty. ■

SECTION 6

The Leaders We Require in 2016

SECTION 6

⇛ | ⇚

Sorry, Democrats
The GOP Has a Bright Future

For the past several years, there has been a persistent drumbeat in the mainstream press proclaiming the pending demise of the Grand Old Party. Most recently, a *Los Angeles Times* headline proclaimed: "Demographic trends favor Democrats, but GOP could still win in 2016." The *Washington Post* weighed in with its own doom and gloom for the GOP: "Dems Head into 2016 with a Clear Demographic Advantage." The theme of such analysis is that America is changing and the GOP cannot or will not compete for Hispanic, African American, Asian, LGBT, and millennial voters, who will give Democrats a lock on political power in America.

Having lost the popular vote in five out of the past six presidential elections (yes, remember Al Gore won the national popular vote despite losing it in Florida), many Republicans have themselves become pessimistic about their future relevance. Political pros on both sides of the aisle know that even if Mitt Romney had won the exceedingly close states of Florida, Virginia, and Ohio in 2012, he would have still narrowly lost the Electoral College vote to President Obama.

I do not agree with the mainstream pundits or share the pessimism of some of my GOP friends about our party's future for two key

This article was originally published in the *National Interest*, September 2, 2015.

reasons. First, Republicans, from the very foundation of their party, have embraced the idea of individual freedom. I believe that in America, freedom and individual liberty will, in the end, always triumph over class division and collectivism with voters of all stripes. Second, the GOP has produced a bumper crop of young reformist leaders who will shape the politics of this country for a generation.

Election returns broadly interpreted support my view. Although President Obama sits in the White House, the GOP is at high-water mark across country. Republicans control the Senate. The party has its biggest majority in the House of Representatives since 1946. More importantly, there are thirty-one Republicans governors and the GOP holds over 4,100 of the nation's approximately 7,000 state legislative seats. The GOP now controls thirty state legislatures compared to just eleven for the Democrats. It has full control of twenty-three state governments (legislature and governorship) compared to a mere seven for the Democrats.

The GOP is winning and will win in the future because it promotes freedom—freedom from the federal government telling Americans when and where they can get healthcare, freedom from the administration picking winners and losers in the market as it has done with politically connected green energy companies, freedom from Washington regulators overseeing every aspect of the Internet, freedom from big-city bureaucrats trying to stifle Uber, Airbnb, and other sharing economy companies and, overseas, freedom from thugs invading their neighbors or radical Islamic terrorists raping and beheading anyone who does not agree with them, including ethnic minorities, unveiled women, gays, and Christians.

The GOP will begin to win at the presidential level because of its star crop of young reformer leaders, who are generating incredible enthusiasm among voters. The Democrats' first team is comprised of baby boomer politicians—Hillary Clinton, Joe Biden, John Kerry, Bernie Sanders, Jerry Brown, and even Al Gore—all of whom are pushing their stale ideas from the 1970s. The GOP, however, will be led for decades by young stars like Wisconsin Governor Scott Walker, Florida Senator Marco Rubio, Texas Senator Ted Cruz, and Louisiana Governor Bobby Jindal, all of whom are now in their mid-forties. Another crop of young Iraq and Afghanistan veterans, who know national security, have bolstered Republican ranks in the House and Senate: Arkansas Senator Tom Cotton, Iowa Senator Joni

Ernst, Alaska Senator Dan Sullivan, Arizona Congresswoman Martha McSally, and California Congressman Duncan Hunter.

To be certain, the 2016 presidential contest will be challenging for the GOP. The Democrats are good at national elections and will fight to hang on to power with every tool at their disposal. Nevertheless, a message of freedom at home and abroad delivered by a new generation of Republican leaders can turn the tide at the presidential level and return to the Grand Old Party to the White House next year. ■

Can Rubio and Cruz Capture the GOP Establishment?

The first two GOP debates have catapulted new candidates into the top tier of the field. In Cleveland, it was Dr. Ben Carson. In Simi Valley, it was Carly Fiorina—who was also following up a "mini-breakout" in Cleveland's undercard debate. Neither candidate "won" the debates so much as they exceeded expectations and subsequently drew real interest from pundits, voters, and fundraisers. Tonight, for the first time, it appears that not one, but two, candidates are poised for breakout performances.

As the Republican presidential candidates prep for tonight's CNBC debate in Boulder, Colorado, the GOP establishment remains deeply nervous as Carson and Donald Trump continue to maintain strong leads in the polls less than one hundred days before Iowa's first-in-the-nation caucuses. The establishment's choices have narrowed as the fall has progressed: Well-respected conservative Governors Scott Walker and Rick Perry exited the race, and Governors John Kasich, Chris Christie, and Jeb Bush remain mired in the low single-digits in the polls. It's not even clear that Christie will make the next main debate stage on November 10.

Instead, the eyes of conservative party regulars are settling on the two candidates, Marco Rubio and Ted Cruz, who have the highest poll

This article was originally published in *Politico Magazine*, October 28, 2015.

numbers of any current or former office holders in the field. Both senators rode the Tea Party wave into the United States Senate in 2010 and 2012, and appear able to bridge the gap between the establishment's desire for stability and governing experience and the base's desire for an "outsider" focused on their core concerns.

Rubio's and Cruz's developing GOP mainstream conservative embrace is consistent with the prediction made by 2012 GOP nominee Mitt Romney back in January when he passed on the 2016 race. Governor Romney said then: "I believe that one of our next generation of Republican leaders, one who may not be as well known as I am today, one who has not yet taken their message across the country, one who is just getting started, may well emerge as being better able to defeat the Democrat nominee."

Given the momentum they are riding into Boulder and based on their past performance and superior debating skills, I predict, with confidence, that Rubio and Cruz will be the winners tonight. They were the best debaters in the previous gatherings in Cleveland and in Simi Valley, California. Not merely expectations-game "best," where the candidates' supporters and media pundits declare winners and losers based on what the candidates "had to do" to stay in the race or who got off the cleverest one-liner at Donald Trump's expense—Rubio and Cruz were actually the best at fluently addressing the issues of importance to the likely caucus and primary voters.

The men appear to have a special blend of GOP DNA: Rubio and Cruz appeal to both the key social conservative and defense hawk wings of GOP with their respective 98 percent and 100 percent lifetime American Conservative Union ratings. They smartly focus on those constituencies in their debate answers. In Cleveland, Rubio said the current generation would be considered "barbarians" by future historians for legalizing abortion. In Simi Valley, he hammered the Obama administration on the Iran nuclear deal and its normalization of diplomatic relations with Cuba. "Clinton will not overturn these deals as president. I will," he said to applause. Federalist Society types, meanwhile, are still talking about Cruz's Simi Valley rebuke of Presidents George H. W. Bush and George W. Bush for selecting Justice David Souter and Chief Justice John Roberts for Supreme Court vacancies over reliably conservative judges Edith Jones and Michael Luttig. Cruz also drew strong applause by flatly declaring he would end the Iran nuclear deal on "day one" of his presidency.

Rubio and Cruz bring with them only-in-America personal stories that rival the "log cabin" narratives of presidential candidates in the nineteenth century. They are Hispanic American children of immigrants. Rubio rode his skill as a high school quarterback to college in Florida, followed by law school. Cruz excelled in debate and earned degrees from Princeton and Harvard Law. They are men of strong religious faith and have beautiful young families. And both men are from that next generation Romney predicted would carry the torch in 2016: Rubio is forty-three years old, Cruz is forty-four.

Together, by heritage, economic circumstances of birth, age, optimism, and ideology, Rubio and Cruz present a stark and positive GOP contrast to the Democratic front-runners—former Secretary of State Hillary Clinton and Senator Bernie Sanders.

To win the nomination, Rubio and Cruz must show the establishment and mainstream Republicans that they are winners. They will not do this by going after each other. Rubio's campaign has run on a financial shoestring. He must convince the donors who have been on the sidelines or who are supporting another establishment candidate that he is their guy. It would not be surprising to see him cordially, but firmly, draw contrasts on the issues and style with Bush, Kasich, and Christie. Rubio may do so on Iran with Bush, who has taken a more nuanced approach to the nuclear deal than the rest of the field. Rubio will attempt to demonstrate to the donor class that he is the only center-right office holder with the ability to go the long haul with the outsiders.

Cruz, for his part, must show the party that the outsider image he has cultivated in the Senate is sufficient to beat Trump and Carson among the base in the upcoming caucus and primary contests. If he can, mainstreamers in the party would forgive and forget any past disagreements on Senate-floor tactics and rally to the Texas senator over the unelected insurgents. Accordingly, Cruz will need to abandon his kid-glove treatment of Trump and Carson and draw contrasts with them tonight. He certainly has an opening to do so on national security versus Trump, who has been playing up how chummy he will be with Vladimir Putin if he is elected.

The field has much uncertainty ahead of it, no matter how tonight unfolds: After Boulder, Trump and Carson may continue to lead in the polls—they are clearly connecting with a wing of the party dissatisfied with the status quo. And no one can predict the impact of an expected and unprecedented nine-figure media buy by Bush's "Right to Rise" super PAC. Fiorina continues to present herself as a real contrast to Hillary Clinton. GOP primary history, however, has shown that strong debate performances in the run-up to Iowa, New Hampshire, South Carolina, and Nevada matter. It is when voters really pay attention to the race. This fact gives Rubio and Cruz a big opening. They both know it. If they are the front-runners come January, it will be a shift that began tonight in Boulder. ■

≋ | ≋

Third Time's the Charm

In early June 1964, a group of Republican governors sought to wrestle control of their party from Barry Goldwater, the Arizona conservative who was about to lead the GOP to one of the most crushing defeats in its history. The governors saw a disaster in the making, and sought a moderate candidate who could capture the imaginations of grassroots Republicans—but also beat President Lyndon Johnson in the general election. Led by Ohio's James Rhodes—the Republican Governors Association was meeting in Cleveland, and Rhodes was a legendary vote counter—the group included Pennsylvania's William Scranton and later New York's Nelson Rockefeller.

When Richard Nixon spurned their advances—after losing to John F. Kennedy in 1960, he had gone on to lose the California governor's race in 1962 and was licking his wounds and perhaps already setting his sights on 1968—the group turned to Michigan's George Romney, who considered the overture and then rejected it. Former President Dwight Eisenhower was on the fringes of the group—pushing but not dictating, afraid that Goldwater's nomination would lead to electoral doom, which it did.

Fast-forward fifty years. Hugh Hewitt and I—both Romney supporters in 2012, with Hewitt openly supporting his election on the air and

This article, co-authored with Hugh Hewitt, was originally published in *Politico Magazine*, September 11, 2014.

me serving as part of the campaign team—repeatedly, indeed inevitably, receive the same question when sitting down with politically active center-right conservatives, especially contributors who drive a lot of the early positioning of the GOP field: "Is Mitt running?"

Neither of us knew anything, and had not talked to the governor about it in the nearly two years since his defeat. He had said "No, no, no, no, no" enough times for us to hear clearly a firm and probably family-wide decision not to seek the 2016 nomination. This resolute rejection of speculation came despite the very strong polling afoot that would make him the prohibitive Republican front-runner amid a weak primary field, a ready-to-go campaign team, a financial network at least as powerful as Hillary Clinton's, and great press from his nonstop, cross-country campaign for GOP candidates at all levels this summer.

But neither of us had asked the man himself. Pressed again and again by friends and colleagues, Hewitt decided to try. He succeeded on Tuesday, August 26, when Governor Romney returned to the air for an interview. Those twenty minutes—and Romney's enigmatic "you know, circumstances can change, but I'm just not going to let my head go there"—sparked more reaction across more and varied platforms than any Hewitt has conducted in the fifteen years his nationally syndicated radio show has been on the air. Among the insider veterans of the 2012 campaign, the enthusiasm for another Romney run went from thirty-five miles per hour to eighty miles per hour, and I fielded numerous calls from the press, former Romney staffers, and major contributors on what the interview meant.

As with all things Romney, he meant what he said—that he thinks there are stronger candidates out there right now, but that circumstances can change. Pundits are left to speculate: What constitutes changed circumstances, and what would Romney do if confronted with the same choice his father faced in 1964? George Romney was a man whose word was his bond. He had committed to Michigan voters that he would finish his term, and that pledge held him back in 1964. No such chain binds Mitt Romney, and a close reading of his remarks on August 26 suggest the 2012 nominee knows his father's history and the consequences of a refusal by a strong nominee to step up when called upon for the good of the party and the country.

Today, we don't know what those changed circumstances are. We do know from our incoming calls that the many sound reasons being offered by his backers—reasons that reach far beyond the polls, fundraising capacity, and the generally 100 percent correct record of predictions Romney made in the fall of 2012 about where the country would be today—continue to fuel the Romney 2016 boom.

Among those arguments:

1. A third run doesn't make a candidate the new "Stassen."

Romney—a man who has always been successful in everything else he does—doesn't want to be seen as repeat failure in politics. He himself referred to the "loser" tag in the Netflix documentary *Mitt*, which opened the eyes of many viewers to a Mitt Romney they had never glimpsed. Gone was the stiff, airbrushed candidate of his critics' caricature; in its place was the real Mitt: a caring father, an earnest patriot, and a warm and funny person.

Certainly, Romney does not want to tarnish his impressive legacy, or his father's, by launching a quixotic 2016 bid. Nor does he want to be the next Harold Stassen, the Minnesota governor who famously ran for president ten times beginning in 1940.

In truth, though, many, many candidates have enjoyed great success with their third run for the presidency (though only five—Richard Nixon, Grover Cleveland, William Henry Harrison, Andrew Jackson, and Thomas Jefferson won the presidency after having earlier been nominated for it and lost). Two more recent twice-nominated GOP candidates deserve our attention:

Thomas Dewey, the governor of New York, ran for president for the first time in 1940 at the age of thirty-eight. He was defeated in his quest for the GOP nomination by Wendell Willkie, who, in turn, lost the general election to President Franklin Roosevelt.

Dewey, following his loss in 1940, received the first of his two GOP nominations for president in 1944. This time, he defeated Willkie in the primaries, and, at the convention, dispatched his chief rival—none other than Harold Stassen. Dewey was defeated in the general election by Roosevelt, of course, but was re-nominated as the GOP standard bearer in 1948 and lost a general election to President Harry Truman that was so close it created an iconic moment in media history: In 1952, while still governor of New York, Dewey supported Eisenhower for president. When Eisenhower briefly considered retiring in 1956, Dewey—whose term had expired two years earlier—was Ike's choice to replace him as president. Eisenhower recovered from health problems and ultimately decided to run again, and Dewey chose to pour his energies into his growing Wall Street law firm. President Lyndon B. Johnson subsequently offered him a seat on the Supreme Court, which Dewey declined in order to remain in private law practice.

Richard M. Nixon, a previous two-time vice-presidential nominee, received his first of two GOP nominations for president in 1960. He was defeated in the general election by John F. Kennedy by a razor-thin margin. Nixon ran for governor of California two years later, only to be defeated by Pat Brown. Dick Nixon's political future was written off by everyone, including Nixon himself—but as early as 1964, party insiders were wooing him back.

Nixon, of course, did come back to win the presidency, albeit narrowly, in 1968. He literally began to reshape the world with his foreign policy achievements and was re-elected in a landslide in 1972. When he resigned the presidency two years later amid the Watergate scandal, he was thought finished on the national and international stage. In his globe-trotting retirement, however, he came to define the label "senior statesman," proving that not just third but fourth and fifth acts are possible in American politics.

In sum, both of these repeat candidates went on to great success—in the private sector in Dewey's case and in the public arena in Nixon's. Neither man was a loser in any sense of the word.

Other major GOP candidates have sought the presidency in multiple campaigns and also found success in their post-third-run lives, even when they did not win:

Harold Stassen is generally held out as the personification of the perennial candidate and the butt of jokes in political circles. (The *Milwaukee Journal* noted a reporter asking at a Stassen press conference in the 1976 campaign: "Q. What politician believes Harold Stassen will be nominated? A. Harold Stassen.") A few Romney foes are already trotting out the Stassen trope. This comparison is as unfair as it is superficial, and considers only Stassen's late-in-life runs—not the four in which he was a serious candidate. A "boy wonder" of American politics, Stassen was elected governor of Minnesota at age thirty-one. His first three quests for the GOP nomination were very serious and credible. In 1944, he was a favorite-son candidate for the GOP nomination but was unable to campaign effectively, as he was serving as a US Navy captain in the Pacific. On his second run, in 1948, he was one of three GOP front-runners, together with Dewey and Senator Robert Taft of Ohio. Stassen defeated Dewey in several primaries and he was Dewey's last major rival at the convention that year.

In 1952, in a third attempt at the nomination, Stassen was one of two GOP front-runners (the other being Taft) until Eisenhower joined the race. Stassen eventually ended his candidacy and supported Ike, serving as one of his chief campaign surrogates in the general election. Following Eisenhower's election, he headed the Foreign Operations Administration and later served as special assistant for disarmament affairs, with cabinet rank. Even in 1964, some GOP voters considered him a palatable alternative to Goldwater.

Only after 1964 did Stassen became a punch line. But he remained active at the national level in his church, holding major positions in the Baptist Convention, and his international law practice in Philadelphia was successful. He retired to Minnesota, and his passing at age ninety-four in 2001 was reported with sympathetic national obituaries. He wasn't a loser.

Ronald Reagan sought the GOP nomination three times, a fact that seems unknown to a younger generation of political pundits (as indeed, most of this history is). In his first national race in 1968, Reagan, then the governor of California, entered the contest late and was easily dispatched by Nixon.

In 1976, Reagan challenged incumbent President Gerald R. Ford for the Republican nomination. In one of the closest GOP nomination races in history, Ford narrowly defeated Reagan at the convention, but it was Reagan who had won the delegates' hearts.

Still, four years later, Reagan's age sent the party on a desperate hunt for an alternative. But he laughed off the speculation about his health and beat a strong field of contenders that included, among others, future President George H. W. Bush, future nominee Bob Dole and a behind-the-scenes effort to draft former President Ford into the race. Obviously, nobody would call Ronald Reagan—still one of America's most popular presidents—a loser.

Bob Dole was the unsuccessful GOP vice-presidential nominee in 1976, running on the ticket with President Ford. He sought the Republican nomination for president the first time in 1980, only to earn less than 1 percent of the vote in the New Hampshire primary before dropping out and urging Ford to enter the race. In 1988, Dole ran for president again. Despite winning the Iowa caucuses and briefly leading the field, he lost the race to Vice President George H. W. Bush.

In 1996, Dole, by then the Senate majority leader, was the early front-runner in the GOP race, his third attempt at the nation's highest office, and went on to win the Republican nomination before losing badly to incumbent President Bill Clinton. Following his defeat, Dole became a lobbyist at an international law firm in Washington and, of course, a beloved figure and spokesman for the Greatest Generation. He has served on many blue-ribbon commissions and is considered one of America's leading senior statesmen by members of both parties. Not a loser.

2. Experience counts. A lot. More than anyone knows.

In *Outliers,* the *New Yorker* writer Malcolm Gladwell asserts, "The closer psychologists look at the careers of the gifted, the smaller the role innate talent seems to play and the bigger the role preparation seems to play." This is the famous "10,000 hours" rule, and—whatever its scientific validity—Romney is a poster boy for it. Maybe he wasn't a natural pol, but after six years of national campaigning, his speeches and rallies in the waning days of the 2012 campaign had a Reaganesque feel. This summer, as he campaigns around the country for GOP congressional candidates, his confidence and skill on the trail are unmatched by anyone other than Barack Obama or Bill Clinton. Presidential campaigning is a learned skill, just like any other. If the candidate keeps growing, the skill set improves. First-timers rarely win the nomination, much less the election. Experience goes a long way.

It's all the more important because Hillary Clinton's presumed cakewalk to the White House is premised on nothing but her and her husband's experience running for the office. They have a machine. It went off the rails in 2008, but only because Obama's ascent was an extraordinary moment in American politics, and perhaps too because Team Clinton assumed too much about Hillary's own inevitability. A 2016 run will, in effect, be Hillary's fourth campaign for 1600 Pennsylvania Avenue. Anyone who tells you a candidate for first lady isn't running for office is not a serious pundit. The staffing, the strategy sessions, the fundraising, the debate prep—all that is almost as much a part of the spouse's life as the candidate's.

Hillary has run three times. This is a huge advantage. She knows the pitfalls. She knows whom to trust and whom to keep at a distance. She knows the media. She may have shown a little rust during her book tour, but come campaign season she will not be making rookie mistakes like forgetting that recording devices are everywhere and always listening.

For Romney, a third run would feature a far more confident and relaxed man—a 10,000-hour candidate. It is a good bet that Hillary fears a Romney three-peat more than she does the first-time national candidacy of any of the other potential GOP nominees.

3. The compressed primary schedule favors Romney. (Or maybe Ted Cruz.)

The pros know that Romney would have a huge advantage in 2016, given how the Republican Party has crunched its debate and primary/caucus schedule, whose long, rolling circus in 2012 was as damaging as it was entertaining—and given the weakness of the GOP field.

Yes, there is the "Ted X" factor. The junior senator from Texas has won the hearts of a large swath of the GOP because he is charismatic, combative, and talented. Ted Cruz's skill set is uniquely ready for a ten- to twelve-debate GOP primary playoff. You don't get to make nine Supreme Court arguments because you are lucky. Cruz has tapped into a deep desire among Republicans to confront the Obama legacy head on, and to fire all torpedoes at once.

Marco Rubio possesses similar rhetorical gifts, and has taken a key role leading the "peace through strength" wing of the party. Although some of the GOP governors eyeing the race have executive experience on their side, presidential nominations are theater, not deliberations, unless they get to a brokered convention—something that has not happened for well over half a century.

But here again, Romney has some advantages. Both Cruz and Rubio would be first-timers, subject to first-time errors and the fear factor so easily generated by a Hillary-enabling mainstream media. (Do you doubt that the media's in the tank for Hillary? See the hard-hitting interviews that marked her book tour.) Further, President Obama's stunning lack of competence in office may unfairly be used against these two highly talented junior senators, who have roughly the same amount of national experience now that Obama did when he ran as a first-term senator in 2008.

And maybe Romney wouldn't even have to formally run. A brokered convention, as Hewitt has written elsewhere, might be within Romney's control to dictate via a limited favorite-son campaign that puts his name into nomination in New Hampshire, Massachusetts, Michigan, Utah, and California—all states where he has lived for long periods of time and accomplished much while living there, as well as the LDS-friendly states of Arizona, Nevada, and Idaho.

But limited or full throttle, Romney would have to say "yes," not "circumstances can change" to set the wheels in motion. And we're not the only ones counseling him to run, by the way. Many others are urging him get in the race, including his 2012 running mate Paul Ryan, Wisconsin Senator Ron Johnson, Utah Representative Jason Chaffetz, and Joe Scarborough of *Morning Joe*. Romney's family is as tightly knit as any we know. Some would love to see him run again; others are ambivalent. They all believe that Mitt would be a great president. If he decided to run again, Ann and his sons would campaign as energetically as ever. But it will be his choice. Although Romney has far more time than any other would-be candidate to announce his entry into the race, at some point following the midterm elections, Romney himself will have to say "go."

What would make him do it? Romney knows the current crop of contenders stands little chance against Hillary. No doubt there are potential candidates—men he respects tremendously—who could give him pause.

These include Ohio Senator Rob Portman, who has been around four score and seven presidential debate preps, and former Florida Governor Jeb Bush. Both, however, have hurdles to plausibility. Governor Bush's attachment to the Common Core education reforms and his position on immigration will draw strong attacks from Cruz and others in the conservative base. As for Portman, though he is a reliable and consistent conservative, his status as a longtime Washington insider could hurt him with primary voters in an anti-Washington cycle.

What about Governors Chris Christie of New Jersey and Rick Perry of Texas? Both were thought to be very strong candidates in the early primary states of New Hampshire and South Carolina, and therefore roadblocks to a Cruz "running the table" moment. Now, no matter how unjust and politicized their persecutions, the pseudo-scandals drew blood, and the wounds will bleed for as long as investigations continue. The media will ensure that question marks hang over both men's political futures unless they can button down those open-ended inquires very soon.

Which brings us back to Cruz. He looks very strong in Iowa—stronger than Iowa's winner in 2008, former Senator Rick Santorum (who, let's acknowledge, never had a real shot at winning the 2012 nomination). Cruz appears to be in at least in second place in New Hampshire (where Senator Rand Paul will have a devoted following of Yankee town-hall veterans who love his style). He probably enjoys a lead in deep-red and Tea Party-friendly South Carolina as well.

And Rubio? Could he hang on until the Florida primary and through the first Super Tuesday on March 1—where all contests must have their delegates proportionately allocated—or the second Super Tuesday on March 15, where the contests can be winner-take-all? Would a late rally to an establishment "not Cruz" candidate split the party too deeply for the disappointed followers of the Texan supernova?

Could that not-Cruz be a re-elected Governor Scott Walker of Wisconsin, or Ohio's ebullient John Kasich? Kasich briefly considered a presidential run in 2000, and no one is as battle-hardened as Walker, though he faces his pesky own legal inquiries by partisan Wisconsin investigators. Both do have big fundraising chops.

Or what about Carly Fiorina? She's almost certainly going to run as well, and who will keep her off the stage even as she drains some votes from the center-right, thereby assisting Cruz?

In his August 26 interview, Romney said he was already "defined" in America's mind, and that this made it hard for him to run, implying a lot of difficult re-branding work, endless explanations and apologies for the "47 percent" comment, and pointing out that Romneycare worked as a limited, one-state exchange and was not the forerunner to the Obamacare fiasco.

But Romney would likely be facing an opponent in Hillary Clinton, whose State Department record is among the worst of all modern cabinet officers, with the terrible toll of her "reset button" mounting by the day. What is she going to tout as her big achievement? Burma?

Just look at the world—what Bill Clinton's Secretary of State Madeleine Albright gently calls "a mess," but which is rather a cauldron of dangers and challenges. It is a far messier world than even the one Reagan faced upon assuming office in 1981. Obama's incompetence will have meant eight years, not Carter's four, to endanger global stability and hollow out America's military.

And Hillary was right there with him. Meanwhile, Romney called every foreign policy fiasco we now face. Every one.

Nor is Hillary, for all her undeniable advantages, made of Teflon. She is brittle in interviews and does not have Mitt's sprightly stride. She has been a Washington fixture since 1993. Romney has never lived there. And Romney at least admits to having money—something he earned it the old-fashioned way by buying and building companies, not by speculating in cattle futures, book deals, speaking engagements, or through the help of unnamed friends and the massively opaque Clinton Foundation.

If any appeal to Romney works, it will be one based on one of two recognitions by him. The first is that patriots are called to difficult things, even incredibly hard things. As Hewitt quoted to him in the recent interview, Thomas Paine wrote in December of 1776, at a low point for the new country, "These are the times that try men's souls. The summer soldier and the sunshine patriot will in this crisis shrink from the service of their country, but he that stands it now deserves the love and thanks of man and woman."

Romney is no summer soldier, but he was very much a governor of Massachusetts, steeped in Revolutionary War writing and argument. Many, especially on the left, will think it corny, but an appeal to Romney's patriotism should not be underestimated. The world really is a disaster, and Romney cares deeply about foreign policy—it's been the focus of much of what he's said and written since 2012. His concern about America's deteriorating global position could be decisive in helping make up his mind.

The second argument is made from his father's record and legacy. George Romney was as good and decent a man as American politics has produced in generations. If the family says to the governor, "Your dad would have run," and they back it up with arguments about why Mitt is the man to rescue his country, circumstances will change very quickly.

If Romney saw that the GOP nomination were going to a candidate even more "defined" than he is and who is far less likely to win, would he feel the fabled sense of duty that animated his father and himself? Would Ann Romney, the boys and their wives, and Romney's close circle of longtime friends be similarly moved?

We've heard Romney's denials, most recently last weekend, when he said, "my time has come and gone." But they are not Shermanesque. He commented to Fox News host Chris Wallace, "I'm not running. I'm not planning on running." This accurately reflects the current status of his thinking and is consistent with his early statement to Hewitt that "circumstances can change." And, it is clearly not General Sherman's famous "I will not accept if nominated, and will not serve if elected." After all, he keeps touring the country, speaking out against President Obama's policies, and inspiring many Republicans who desperately want to win in 2016—and know that he can. Over the past month, numerous current and former Republican officeholders, officials, major contributors, and senior advisers have reached out to Romney by phone and e-mail and urged him to enter the race. They are staying on the sidelines until they are certain he will not run, which may be as late as next winter.

Imagine one interview from Romney, in which he says something like: "Circumstances can change, I'm best positioned to win, and the GOP nominee has to win—simply has to win. For the free world. For the Supreme Court. For people looking to protect their children's futures. And, especially, for the men and women in uniform who deserve a commander-in-chief who will respect them, properly equip them, and lead them—from where America has always led—the front."

Couple that interview or statement with the real Mitt Romney—the one from the documentary—speaking to the nation from the heart every day and on every stop. Match that Mitt against the polished and calculating Hillary Clinton. Well then, as Paul Ryan said, the third time really could be the charm. Romney may still do this: 2016 needs Mitt even if Mitt doesn't think he needs it—yet. ■

EPILOGUE

The world in 2016 is a very dangerous place. Winston Churchill's great-grandson, Jonathan Sandys, said that if Sir Winston "were on Twitter today, he would be shouting against this deal with Iran and saying that this is the second most unwise thing we have ever done, the first being allowing Hitler to rise. And he would be warning the world to sit up and wake up." I made a similar point in my essay, "What Would Churchill Do?"

The threat from Islamic jihadists has grown dramatically since President Bush left office. Non-state actors such as the Islamic State and al-Qaeda have both launched and inspired attacks in the West— Paris, San Bernardino, and Brussels being examples of both types of assaults. The Islamic State has seized and held ground in Iraq and Syria, establishing a Salafist caliphate the size of Britain, to which it can draw jihadists from around the world and from which it can plan and launch attacks against the West. On the Shia side of the coin, the Islamic Republic of Iran is the largest state sponsor of terrorism in the world and is building an archipelago across the Middle East using proxies and Revolutionary Guard forces from Yemen to Syria to Lebanon. Such extremism, whether Salafist or Shia, is a long-term threat to America and its allies. The UK Ministry of Defense Strategic Trends Programme predicts that "by 2035 extreme religious networks [read: jihadists] are likely to be increasingly global and will often play a greater role in channeling transnational support to ideologically-driven conflicts."

Peak political correctness in the West prevents governments from even identifying, much less fighting, an ideological war against the jihadists. A lack of political will to commit sufficient armed forces to defeat the Islamic State, or to confront and deter Iran, mean that this threat will not be adequately addressed without a new administration and a new national security policy in Washington. Meanwhile, millions of migrants, primarily military-aged young men from North Africa and the Middle East, stream into Europe—a circumstance that will change the security environment, culture, and demography of the continent forever.

As the West grapples with the global war on terror (even though that term has been banished by the Obama administration), our near peer competitors, Russia and China, have embarked on massive defense buildups. Having watched America and its allies project power and defeat adversaries over long distances for almost forty years—from the Falklands to first Gulf War, and from Yugoslavia to the second Gulf War—our adversaries have learned important lessons. Russia and, especially, China have developed anti-access and area denial (A2/AD) tactics and platforms to keep America and NATO out of their neighborhoods. Anti-ship ballistic missiles such as China's Dong Feng 21 put American carriers at risk much farther out to sea than has ever before been the case. Supersonic anti-ship cruise missiles, ultra-quiet diesel-electric submarines, super-cavitating torpedoes, anti-satellite weapons, and cyber warfare capabilities are all part of the Russian and Chinese toolkit to deny expeditionary forces access to contested areas near their territories.

The point of the Russian and Chinese buildups is to give those nations the freedom to operate against their neighbors, even American friends, with impunity. Russia's annexation of the Crimea and state-sponsored civil war in Ukraine is well known. Its carve-up of Georgia and Moldova has been less widely reported. Success in those adventures may only encourage Moscow to attempt to reassert control or "Finlandize" the Baltic States, all three of which are members of NATO.

China has asserted sovereignty over the entire South China Sea and enforces its writ by occupying islands and reefs that are far closer to Hanoi and Manila than to the Chinese coastline. In the East China Sea, China seeks to wrest control of the Senkaku Islands from Japan. China now even claims sovereignty over the Ryukyu island chain. Those islands include Okinawa, home to a major United States Marine Corps installation, not to mention thousands of Japanese citizens. America's response to Russian aggression and Chinese assertiveness has been feeble.

Regional power Iran and pariah state North Korea have also adopted an A2/AD approach by developing or purchasing the necessary weapons, including sophisticated anti-aircraft missiles from Russia. Iran and North Korea have also developed significant ballistic missile programs, giving them the means to deliver weapons of mass effect, even nuclear warheads, over long distances. Much of this technology has found its way to Pakistan, which itself is under assault from the Taliban, putting such weapons almost within the grasp of Islamic terrorists.

All of these developments give rise to many possible deadly scenarios that could unfold on the next president's watch. Unfortunately, the resources he or she will have at hand are not what they once were. Sequestration has left America with a military that is close to the post-Vietnam hollow force in terms of readiness and equipment. President Obama's apology tours and "lead from behind" foreign policy have emboldened our adversaries and disheartened our friends. America's engine of success—its economy—has been strangled by executive orders and federal regulation run amok. Thus, the next president must rebuild all of America's national capabilities—economic, military, and diplomatic—with speed. Fortunately, we know from the 1980s that it can be done.

A quote attributed to Chancellor Bismarck shortly before his death supposes that "God has a special providence for drunkards, fools, and the United States of America." There is no question that America is blessed with amazing and innovative people, who have shown their hope for the future by not falling into the declining population trap that has affected much of the developed world. As Stratfor's George Friedman regularly points out, America's geography—protected by vast oceans, bordered by friendly neighbors, abundant in oil, gas, minerals, and farmland, and layered with navigable rivers—is the foundation of American power. I posit that while demography and geography may be destiny, the true greatness of America is found in its ideology—not an ideology of state power found in the "isms," but in a belief in individual freedom and liberty underpinned by the rule of law. That idea is perhaps best captured in the second stanza of "America the Beautiful," which asks our citizens to "confirm thy soul in self-control, thy liberty in law!"

Compared to Russia, China, Iran, the Islamic State caliphate, North Korea, Venezuela, or Cuba, the United States and its allies remain in remarkable shape and should triumph under any circumstance. Only a decision to continue to retreat from the world stage and to transform our way of life and military could lead to defeat. Building upon the clear advantages the United States enjoys, the next president can turn the tide of affairs by taking a path very different than the present one, which sadly has an uncomfortable similarity to the path that lead to the fateful events of 1938.

First, he or she must be committed to a national security policy of "peace through strength." Rebuilding our military will require determination and funding. The equipment and platforms developed during the Reagan years are in many cases over thirty years old. The six-hundred-ship fleet is down to 272 ships and falling. The bomber wing of the air force relies on B-52s that, if they were people, would be the grandparents of their current pilots. The Army is too small to accomplish its missions. The Marine Corps is in the same situation and lacks the requisite number of amphibious ships and "connectors" to get them to shore in a conflict. The Coast Guard is down to one ice-breaker at a time when the arctic is turning into a key strategic shipping lane.

Rebuilding America's defenses is a complicated mosaic beyond the scope of this essay. It must include, however, the following elements:

The acquisition process must be radically reformed and the Pentagon's purchasing bureaucracy must be trimmed. Technology is moving too quickly for the armed forces to wait ten years for new weapons platforms.

The US Navy must have at least 350 warships to maintain presence in the global commons. Those ships must be capable of defending themselves in surface combat with near-peer competitor navies. The fleet should include at least twelve large-deck Nimitz- and Ford-class carriers. Those carriers require a long-range naval aviation strike capability not currently in the fleet. The Navy or Coast Guard must be provisioned with both ice-breakers and arctic patrol vessels that are robust and sufficiently armed to defend US interests in the polar regions.

The Air Force requires a long-range strike bomber (LRSB) built in sufficient numbers to provide a credible nuclear deterrent and to provide conventional punch in an A2/AD environment. The F-35 Lightning II, despite its controversial development issues, must also be built in sufficient numbers to replace current squadrons of F-15s, F-16s and A-10s. The curtailment of the B-2 Spirit and F-22 Raptor programs, which left the Air Force with far too few of both planes, cannot be repeated with the LRSB and F-35.

The Army and Marine Corps have been reduced to a state where fighting two simultaneous regional wars would be close to impossible. Even under current deployments, the men and women of the Army and Marine Corps are being stretched to the breaking point. The Army should, at a minimum, have seventy combat brigades and 520,000 active duty soldiers, as former Secretary of Defense Robert Gates recommended. The Marine Corps should, at a minimum, have three active and one reserve Marine Expeditionary Forces and 225,000 active and reserve Marines in the Corps, again as recommended by Secretary Gates.

Second, the next president must reassert American leadership. America used to be considered the leader of the free world. It is very rare to hear that term used any longer. It should be used—and we should be proud of it. Being the leader of the free world does not mean being the policeman of the entire world. It does mean that America should use its moral authority to promote the idea of free men and women and free markets for the betterment of the world.

Like rebuilding our defenses, rebuilding our alliances is critical. The next president should fly Air Force One to Tel Aviv and meet the Israeli prime minister at his office in Jerusalem as his or her first foreign trip as president. Mitt Romney intended to do this had he been elected. It would send a message not just to the Middle East but also to our allies throughout the world that America is a reliable friend. Our closest and most militarily capable ally is the United Kingdom, which has fought with America in the two great wars of the twentieth century, Korea, the Gulf Wars, Yugoslavia, and Afghanistan. No American president should refer to the Falkland Islands as "Las Malvinas," as President Obama did while trying to curry favor with Bolivarians during a visit to South America.

NATO is the most successful military alliance in history. Under American leadership, our NATO allies must be encouraged to invest in their own defense. Ending sequestration here should be an example to those allies. It is also time to consider a global freedom alliance for those tried and true countries that ascribe to the rule of law and are willing to fight to defend freedom. In addition to current NATO members, candidates for such an alliance include, among others, Australia, New Zealand, Japan, Mexico, Colombia, Singapore, Israel, the Philippines and, potentially, India as it sheds its non-aligned ideology and moves away from its weapons purchasing relationship with Russia. Such a bloc would be a powerful force in maintaining the international norms that have given the world such prosperity since the end of World War II.

Third, the American economy is the engine of free-world growth and will sustain the rebuilding of American defenses. The economy must be released from the shackles of over-regulation, punitive corporate taxation that keep profits from US companies stranded overseas, politically motivated permitting decisions (such the administration's refusal to allow the Keystone pipeline to be built), and Obamacare and other government mandates that kill jobs. The safety net must be reformed with bipartisan compromises that ensure a secure retirement for Americans and basic services for those in need. Without such reform, entitlements and debt service will eventually consume the entire federal budget, leaving nothing to defense or other governmental functions. With pro-growth policies like those instituted by President Reagan, America will have the resources necessary to defend itself and to lead the free world.

Based on the 2016 campaign and past four years, it seems that only a Republican president will take the steps required for America to change its present course. Donald Trump's foreign policy positions are not entirely clear, but he has centered his campaign around a Reaganesque promise to "make America great again." Democratic front-runner Hillary Clinton, on the other hand, recently told Fareed Zakaria that she "largely agreed" with President Obama's foreign policy. In the primaries, Clinton has been quick to emphasize her ties to President Obama. One Democratic bright spot is Michèle Flournoy, a likely Secretary of Defense in a Clinton administration, who has called for increased defense spending. While Senator Sanders has said little in the campaign about foreign affairs and national security, he continually points out that he voted against the second Gulf War. A self-described socialist who has built his campaign message around income inequality, there is little doubt that he would seek further defense cuts to fund his domestic spending priorities.

The challenges that America faces and that are outlined in this book are indeed grave. They can, however, be overcome. Indeed, it is still possible to deal with them before they become problems so great as to lead to the type of cataclysmic events that marred the twentieth century. Appeasement and retreat, however, are not the answer. History has taught that such a path, while being both easy and popular at the outset, "is only the first sip, the first foretaste of a bitter cup which will be proffered to us year by year."

America faces a stark choice in 2016 between a continuation of President Obama's "lead from behind" foreign policy and sequester-based national security approach and a return to President Reagan's "leader of the free world" foreign policy and "peace through strength" national security approach. The stakes in this dangerous time could not be higher.

ACKNOWLEDGMENTS

I am grateful to the many people involved in bringing this book to fruition. My publisher, Roger Kimball, and Encounter Books were willing to invest in a first-time author, which I truly appreciate. Keith Urbahn and his top-notch team at Javelin are supportive and creative agents.

Hugh Hewitt encouraged this project from its inception and has been exceedingly generous with his review of various drafts, thoughtful suggestions on arranging the chapters, and in writing the foreword to the book. He co-authored the Politico piece that appears on page 141.

Over the course of the past seven years, colleagues and editors at numerous publications have contributed their excellent insight to each of the essays in the book. Senator Jim Talent, Fox News contributor Richard Grenell, Ambassador Kim Beazley, Harry Kazianis, former editor of the *National Interest*, and Mike Gallagher, who co-wrote the article that formed part of the introduction to this book, all merit special recognition and thanks. My secretary, Gladys Madrid, and intern, Dane Cummaro, were very diligent in assisting me with the manuscript.

President George W. Bush allowed me to work with the State Department as his appointee in various capacities during most of his second term, for which I am grateful. His leadership after the September 11 attack on our homeland, and his courage in ordering the surge in Iraq that brought us victory, are now part of America's story.

During my career I have had the opportunity to work closely with Ambassador John Bolton, Governor Mitt Romney, Governor Scott Walker, and Senator Ted Cruz on foreign policy and national security matters. Governor Pete Wilson has been a mentor to me since I was an eighteen-year-old intern in Washington. They are all patriots and each of them would make a great President of the United States. I have learned more from them than any counsel that I may have provided.

Two ambassadors with whom I worked have passed away in recent years. Ambassador Rich Williamson would have been a first-rate Secretary of State in the next GOP administration. Ambassador Tom Schweich knew as much about Afghanistan as anyone in the State Department. Both men had many contributions still to offer. They were too young to go and will be missed.

US District Judge David Carter has been a mentor on the rule of law at home and abroad. When the Marines say they want "a few good men," they got one in decorated First Lieutenant Dave Carter, who served with courage and distinction at Khe Sanh in Vietnam.

My law partners and colleagues have encouraged and supported my professional, foreign policy, and political endeavors over the years. My partner at Larson O'Brien LLP, Judge Stephen Larson (ret.), is one of the best trial attorneys in America. I would not try a case without Steve Bledsoe at my side. Ambassador Pierre Prosper is a formidable diplomat and has been a terrific travel companion to faraway locales. And, of course, I owe a tremendous debt of gratitude to the many clients who have entrusted their legal representation to me over the years.

I have been the beneficiary of too many courtesies and too much counsel from colleagues in government, campaigns, and in the law to properly acknowledge in this space—but those who have extended them to me should know of my deep appreciation.

Any success that I have achieved is properly credited to my wife, Lo-Mari, who has been a sounding board, editor, trusted advisor, and best friend since we met in a political science class in 1987. Her steadfast support and many sacrifices over the course of a professional and political career that has involved too many late nights and too much travel has made all the difference to me and our three children, Margaret, Robert Christopher, and Lauren. Robert Christopher wanted me to write this book. Heartbreakingly, we lost him in a tragic accident in September 2015. It is to him that this work is dedicated.

My parents, Bob and Judy, are at the root of this. My earliest political memories include heading out in the family station wagon to welcome Richard Nixon home to California at El Toro Marine Corps Air Station in Orange County on August 9, 1974, and attending a rally for Ronald Reagan two summers later during his second run for the GOP nomination. I cannot thank my parents and brother and sister, Patrick and Kelley, enough for their love, support, and encouragement.

Just five years after the 1976 Reagan rally, my California Teenage Republican co-founder and current St. Francis Winery CEO, Christopher Silva, and I were in the Rose Garden with President Reagan. In 1984, I was an intern at the Republican National Committee in Washington and a page at the Republican National Convention in Dallas where President Reagan was re-nominated. It truly was "morning in America" that summer. Just as I am certain President Reagan would be if he were still with us, I remain confident that notwithstanding these troubled times, America's best days lie ahead. I thank God for the blessing of having been born here.

INDEX

ABOUT THE AUTHOR

Robert C. O'Brien is a trial lawyer with an international practice at Larson O'Brien LLP in Los Angeles. He was a senior foreign policy advisor to Governor Scott Walker and Senator Ted Cruz during the 2016 presidential campaign. O'Brien served as a senior advisor to Governor Mitt Romney on both of his presidential campaigns.

O'Brien was Co-Chairman of the US Department of State Public-Private Partnership for Justice Reform in Afghanistan. He served as a presidentially appointed member of the US Cultural Property Advisory Committee. In 2005, O'Brien was nominated by President George W. Bush and confirmed by the Senate to serve as a US Representative to the United Nations General Assembly, where he worked with Ambassador John Bolton. Earlier in his career, O'Brien was a senior legal officer with the United Nations Security Council in Geneva, Switzerland. He served as a major in the JAG Corps of the US Army Reserve.

A frequent guest on Fox News, *The Hugh Hewitt Show*, CNN, and other radio and cable TV networks, O'Brien is regularly called upon by the media to interpret and comment on breaking national security and political stories.

He lives in Southern California with his wife and children.